A British Eyewitness
AT THE
Battle of New Orleans

A British Eyewitness
AT THE
Battle of New Orleans

THE MEMOIR OF
ROYAL NAVY ADMIRAL
ROBERT AITCHISON,
1808–1827

EDITED BY
Gene A. Smith

PUBLISHED BY
THE HISTORIC NEW ORLEANS COLLECTION
2004

The Historic New Orleans Collection is a museum, research center, and publisher dedicated to the study and preservation of the history and culture of New Orleans and the Gulf South region. The Collection is operated by the Kemper and Leila Williams Foundation, a Louisiana nonprofit corporation.

Library of Congress Cataloging-in-Publication Data

Aitchison, Robert, 1795-1861.
A British eyewitness at the Battle of New Orleans : the memoir of Royal Navy Admiral Robert Aitchison, 1808-1827 / edited by Gene A. Smith.— 1st ed.
        p. cm.
Includes bibliographical references and index.
ISBN 0-917860-50-0 (pbk. : alk. paper)
1. Aitchison, Robert, 1795-1861. 2. New Orleans, Battle of, New Orleans, La., 1815—Personal narratives, British. 3. United States—History—War of 1812—Naval operations, British. 4. Sailors—Great Britain—Biography. 5. Great Britain. Royal Navy—Biography. 6. Admirals—Great Britain—Biography. I. Smith, Gene A., 1963- II. Title.
        E356.N5A38 2004
        973.5'239—dc22   2004018563

© 2004 by The Historic New Orleans Collection
533 Royal Street
New Orleans, Louisiana 70130
www.hnoc.org

First edition. 2,000 copies
All rights reserved
Printed by Transcontinental Printing

Priscilla Lawrence, *Executive Director*
Jessica Dorman, *Director of Publications*
Jan White Brantley, *Head of Photography*

Book design and production by Michael Ledet Art & Design, Hammond, Louisiana
Print production management by Kaye Alexander, Westford, Vermont
Typography by Eugenie Seidenberg Delaney, North Ferrisburgh, Vermont
Color scans by Garrison Digital Color, New Orleans, Louisiana
Printed in Canada

Cover illustration: *Battle of Lake Borgne by Thomas L. Hornbrook. The Historic New Orleans Collection (1950.54)*

ACKNOWLEDGMENTS

*E*DITING ROBERT AITCHISON'S MEMOIR has been a demanding but rewarding experience, which never would have been completed without the help of many others. Dean Mary L. Volcansek of AddRan College has steadfastly encouraged my scholarship and rewarded me for my accomplishments. Many history department colleagues at TCU, especially Kenneth Stevens, have been very gracious with their support, time, and advice; biologist Joseph Britton and geologist John Breyer helped answer technical questions. Alan Giddings, formerly of the National Maritime Museum in Greenwich and now a researcher at the International Red Cross, London, shared his expertise and resources—his help was critical in identifying the many obscure British naval officers Aitchison encountered. Likewise, David Taylor of the Picture Library, Centre for Maritime Research at the National Maritime Museum; Clare Freestone of the National Portrait Gallery, London; and Olive Geddes of the National Library of Scotland provided hard-to-find documents and images that complemented Aitchison's story. *The Gazetteer for Scotland*, http://www.geo.ed.ac.uk/scotgaz/, was an invaluable resource. And Helen Mound of Tenbury Wells, Worcestershire, a descendant of Aitchison's brother George, generously shared family papers, photographs, and lore.

Several people at The Historic New Orleans Collection made Herculean contributions to this undertaking: Former director of publications Patricia Brady saw the importance of Aitchison's memoir and envisioned what the book could become; former acting director of publications Louise Hoffman patiently guided the project through turbulent waters and lean times; current director Jessica Dorman has seen the project through to completion, gently prodding a sometimes recalcitrant editor/author to make changes that ultimately created a better book; THNOC executive director Priscilla Lawrence has cheerfully supported my contributions to The Collection; Alfred Lemmon, director of the Williams Research Center, went above and beyond the call of duty, as always; Jason Wiese, with additional assistance from Michael Redman, diligently transcribed the memoir, thereby saving me invaluable time; along with Lynn Adams and Mary Mees, Jason also made important and extensive editorial contributions that have greatly improved the book; Pamela Arcenaux helped to proofread and correct the manuscript; and Jan White Brantley, head of photography, provided excellent visual materials. Michael Ledet of Michael Ledet Art & Design laid out and designed the finished product. Without the support of the board of directors and the help and encouragement of The Historic New Orleans Collection, this project never would have been accomplished.

Finally, my wife, Tracy, and our son Banning Allen Franklin are part of every project that I undertake. While their names do not appear on the title page, their imprint is always present.

Gene A. Smith
Fort Worth, Texas
July 2004

EDITORIAL METHOD

$\mathcal{M}$Y JOB AS EDITOR was to prepare Robert Aitchison's memoir for publication without damaging the historical value or flavor of the original text. As the work advanced, the project became increasingly difficult. Aitchison wrote the memoir in the 1850s and obviously suffered from lapses in memory; the writing worsens as the manuscript progresses, and the narrative ends abruptly without any sense of closure. Throughout, there are indecipherable words, phrases that make little or no sense, and margin notes that do not coincide with the narrative. My goal was to make this mid-nineteenth-century text intelligible to modern readers—preserving the form and effect of Aitchison's original while contextualizing the story as best as possible.

The major editorial tasks were to divide the memoir into chapters, provide better paragraphing to break up the manuscript's density, and identify the often obscure people and places mentioned in the text. Although Aitchison was careless about punctuation and spelling—and imprecise about dates, times, ranks, and titles—the transcription preserves the original text literally, with the following exceptions. The first letter of each sentence has been capitalized; run-on sentences have been broken into less unwieldy (and more grammatical) components; terminal dashes have been changed to periods; dropped apostrophes have been added; superscript characters have been brought down to the line with a period; abbreviated honorifics and military ranks have been spelled out; and the names of naval vessels have been italicized. Brackets, indicating editorial intervention, have been used sparingly to clarify puzzling references and note the placement of marginalia.

Aitchison kept a running chronological tab in the margin of his memoir. Notations of months and years have been included in the transcription only on first mention and at the beginning of chapters—and have been placed at paragraph's start, unless the key transition falls midway through the paragraph.

Following Aitchison's memoir is much like opening a surprise gift—one never knows what to expect in the next sentence. The narrative meanders from one topic to another, often without signposts for the reader. The author introduces individuals and events and then quickly leaves them, without ever mentioning them again. This random stream of thought suggests that Aitchison's memoir was a work in progress, perhaps intended as a first draft to be corrected later. Yet despite its drawbacks as a work of literature, the memoir stands as a precious historical document—a primary source that asks its readers, as it has asked its editor, to drop certain preconceptions about the past and yield to the sway of Robert Aitchison's memories.

CONTENTS

INTRODUCTION

An Average Life in an Uncommon Day

ROBERT AITCHISON'S MEMOIR, penned nearly 150 years ago, recalls an era of unparalleled heroism and human sacrifice—a time when Napoleon schemed for world domination and Britain and the United States met, for the final time, as battlefield opponents. During this epoch hundreds of thousands of young men lost their lives in the struggles to redraw the boundaries of the world map; most left no personal imprint on history. Robert Aitchison—a young naval officer who dodged alligators, shipwreck, and musket shot, all before his twentieth birthday—could well have become another nameless casualty of war. But he survived, and while in his early sixties, he sat down to memorialize his youthful adventures, creating an account that bears little resemblance to textbook history. Aitchison's story does not concern itself with official proclamations or military strategy. Instead, it describes the experiences of an average young man who came of age during uncommon times.

Aitchison's story is particularly compelling for its ability to straddle, and illuminate, two disparate worlds: Britain in the midst of a titanic struggle with France, and the United States trying to define itself as an independent nation. If the operations and activities of the Royal Navy dominate the foreground of Aitchison's memoir, the American landscape (from the coast of Maine to the mouth of the Mississippi) provides the backdrop. Aitchison not only witnessed, but later chronicled, one of the landmark events in American history—the Battle of New Orleans. And while the literature on this dramatic episode is rich and varied, the British eyewitness perspective has been underrepresented; the shameful result of the battle, coupled with the death of Britain's senior commanding officers, reduced not only the British market for firsthand accounts but also the pool of likely authors. Robert Aitchison—a young Scotsman positioned on the margins of battle and the margins of the naval officer class—saw the military debacle and later was free to say what his superiors could not.

Robert Aitchison served throughout the Mediterranean and along the coast of North America. He participated in two important British military engagements—the humiliating New Orleans campaign of 1814-15 and the glorious Battle of Algiers in 1816. Aitchison's service did not set him apart from others of his rank, status, or age. In fact, he was, in many ways, a typical young officer who served King and Country dutifully, receiving little or no credit for the role he played in extending and defending the empire. And, like so many others, he found himself unemployed once the period of intense warfare ended, discarded by the same military system that earlier had welcomed his services. But Aitchison had certain advantages that set him apart from other junior officers. First, he had a powerful patron in Admiral Sir David Milne, a family friend under whom he served in the Mediterranean and along the coast of North America. Milne's advocacy helped Aitchison secure promotion, and employment, in the postwar navy. Second, Aitchison benefited from powerful literary influences, including his maternal grandfather James Mylne (a farmer-poet inspired by Robert Burns) and his older brother John (an ensign in the Scots Guards whose letters home kept the family apprised of Wellington's campaigns). Robert Aitchison appreciated the potency of words. Taking stock of his life, in late middle age, he surely knew that his had not been an exemplary career. He had not shaped the times in which he lived, but with his memoir, he could—and he does—shape our understanding of those times.[1]

A Second War for American Independence

Robert Aitchison's memoir reaches its climax at the Battle of New Orleans. Having insinuated himself ("by hook or by crook") into the ser-

---

1 Maurice Lindsay, "James Mylne," *The Burns Encyclopedia* ([Edinburgh]: Burns Country, 1990s), http://www.robertburns.org/encyclopedia/MylneJamesd1788.672 .shtml; John Aitchison, *An Ensign in the Peninsular War: The Letters of John Aitchison*, ed. W. F. K. Thompson (London, 1981).

vice of Rear Admiral Edward Codrington, Aitchison hauled guns, built breastworks, ferried troops across the Mississippi, and watched as "murderous fire" erupted from the American ranks. Aitchison considered the battle "a disastrous affair from beginning to end"; some historians consider it the final chapter of the American Revolution. Why the Revolution concluded at Chalmette in 1815 and not at Yorktown in 1781 is a matter of some complexity and debate.

The Treaty of Paris, signed in 1783, failed to ameliorate tensions between the United States and Great Britain. The British government granted Americans their independence but continued to treat the United States as a de facto colony; Americans took every British slight as an insult to national honor. Bluster and fiery rhetoric dominated public and diplomatic discourse. But even as taunts and accusations flew, the two nations engaged in pragmatic debates over land and boundaries, neutral and maritime rights, and relations with Native Americans—with both sides hopeful that diplomacy, and legislation, might prevent another war.[2]

European power struggles also intensified the tumult of America's post-Revolutionary period. France declared war on Britain in 1793 and the conflict—continuing intermittently until 1815—tested the patience and neutrality of the United States. Desperate for supplies, and watchful for deserters, both Britain and France persisted in seizing American ships and sailors. The United States retaliated first against France, entering into an undeclared naval conflict (the Quasi-War) in the Caribbean in 1798, but these hostilities were short-lived. The Treaty of Mortefontaine (1800) and the Louisiana Purchase (1803) signaled a diplomatic détente between the U.S. and France, leaving Great Britain to bear the focus of American resentment.[3]

Both the Jefferson and Madison administrations hoped to prompt Britain into respecting American neutrality by applying economic pressure. But none of the legislative restrictions passed by Congress—the

---

2 Reginald Horsman, *The Causes of the War of 1812* (Philadelphia, 1962), 17-23.

3 Bradford Perkins, ed., *The Causes of the War of 1812: National Honor or National Interest?* (New York, 1962), 1-7.

Non-Importation Act of 1806, the Embargo Act of 1807, the Non-Intercourse Act of 1809, or Macon's Bill No. 2 of 1810—had the desired effect. Tensions reached a peak during the summer of 1807, when HMS *Leopard* fired on the U.S. frigate *Chesapeake* off the coast of Virginia, killing three and wounding eighteen. The affair produced great consternation in the United States, but still, no war.[4]

Another set of players further complicated the situation in North America—the Native American tribes whose loyalty, and manpower, the European powers courted. The Old Northwest Territory, bounded to the south by the Ohio River and to the west by the Mississippi, proved a crucial staging ground in the buildup to the War of 1812. Britain retained military posts in the Northwest and continued providing support to Native Americans in the region. The British hoped that an Indian state, or buffer zone, would act as a safeguard against American incursions into Canada. With a loyal Indian fighting force in place, Britain could reallocate its own regiments to other vulnerable spots within the empire. Moreover, an Anglo/Native American alliance would allow the Crown to retain strategic and economic control over important fur-trading lands to the south and west of the Great Lakes.[5]

American expansionism into the Old Northwest strained alliances and bred conflict. In August 1794, U.S. forces under General Anthony Wayne defeated a confederacy of tribes at the Battle of Fallen Timbers; the British, stationed nearby at Fort Miami, failed to provide fallback support for the Indians. The defeat had profound ramifications: the Treaty of Greenville, signed in 1795, ceded much of present-day Ohio to the Americans. Still, the northern tribes turned to the Crown for supplies and encouragement, anticipating that their British "father," King George III, would continue to back them in their struggle against the Americans. But the king, his attentions increasingly diverted by the war in Europe, and his

---

4 Spencer C. Tucker and Frank T. Reuter, *Injured Honor: The Chesapeake-Leopard Affair, June 22, 1807* (Annapolis, 1996), 1-17.
5 Bradford Perkins, *Prologue to War: England and the United States, 1805-1812* (Berkeley, 1961), 95-96, 285-86; Horsman, *Causes of the War of 1812*, 16-17.

sanity increasingly muddled, would never again provide the support they craved.[6]

The Americans, for their part, pursued an increasingly aggressive policy against the British. Congressional "War Hawks"—their ranks swelled by the midterm elections of 1810—pushed for the acquisition of Canadian and western Native American lands, with some even arguing for expansion into Spanish East and West Florida. An intense American Anglophobia, created by years of humiliation at the hands of Great Britain, and an agricultural depression further fanned the war fever. The hawks argued that war might redress national slights and revive the sagging U.S. economy. On June 1, 1812, President Madison asked Congress for a declaration of war; on June 18, he signed off on the proclamation. The stage was set for America's second war for independence—and for Robert Aitchison's brush with history.[7]

"What part I acted in these juvenile days"

Born in 1795, Robert Aitchison spent his early years in the coastal region east of Edinburgh, Scotland. The town of Musselburgh, where the Aitchison family settled, counted just over 4,000 citizens at the time of Robert's birth. An old Scottish rhyme reveals the town's attitude toward its big-city neighbor: *Musselburgh was a burgh when Edinburgh was nane / And Musselburgh will be a burgh when Edinburgh has gane.* Robert's father, William, was descended from a well-connected family of distillers; he

---

6 Reginald Horsman, "British Indian Policy in the Northwest, 1807-1812," *Mississippi Valley Historical Review* 45 (June 1958): 51-66.

7 James D. Richardson, ed., *A Compilation of the Messages and Papers of the Presidents, 1789-1897*, vol. 1, 1789-1817 (Washington, DC, 1896), 499-505; Frank L. Owsley, Jr., and Gene A. Smith, *Filibusters and Expansionists: Jeffersonian Manifest Destiny, 1800-1821* (Tuscaloosa, 1997); Louis M. Hacker, "Western Land Hunger and the War of 1812: A Conjecture," *Mississippi Valley Historical Review* 10 (March 1924): 365-95; Julius Pratt, "Western Aims in the War of 1812," *Mississippi Valley Historical Review* 12 (June 1925): 36-50; Reginald Horsman, "Western War Aims, 1811-1812," *Indiana Magazine of History* 53 (March 1957): 1-18; Margaret K. Latimer, "South Carolina— A Protagonist of the War of 1812," *American Historical Review* 61 (July 1956): 914-29.

Drummore was the Aitchison family home in Musselburgh, Scotland, overlooking the Firth of Forth. Photograph courtesy of George McLeod, Midlothian Historical Society, Scotland

worked as a baker in his early years and married Jane Mylne in 1782, when he was twenty-nine and she was eighteen. In 1808 the Aitchisons purchased the Drummore estate, overlooking the Firth of Forth; their move into the manor house cemented their status as one of the leading families of the area.[8]

Robert was the seventh of eight children born to William and Jane. The oldest of his siblings, William (1784-1846), rose to the rank of colonel in the Scots Fusilier Guards before inheriting Drummore from his father. James (1787-1886) entered business and settled at Alderston estate in nearby Haddington. John (1789-1875), who served in the peninsular wars, attained generalship in the Guards and was later knighted. Helen (1789-1851), the only daughter, was John's twin. George (1791-1847) later became a prosperous merchant, owning and operating four ships for the British East India Company. Francis (1794?-1860) managed family property near Spitalhaugh, Peeblesshire, southwest of Edinburgh. And David (1802-1879), Robert's little brother, became an

Episcopal archdeacon and a major force behind the founding of Christ
Church in Glasgow.[9]

In December 1808, Robert's father secured him a royal appointment
as a first-class naval volunteer, thereby affording him the future opportunity to become a deck officer. Robert's maternal uncle John Rennie—an
eminent engineer who had designed and built docks at Hull, Liverpool,
and Leith, and improved naval dockyards at Chatham, Portsmouth, and
Plymouth—undoubtedly greased the skids for Robert's appointment.
And while Robert's age—just thirteen—may strike present-day readers
as frightfully young for military service, it would not have appeared so to
his contemporaries. Starting at a paltry salary of £7 per annum, Robert
spent the next seven years learning the operations of naval vessels and
the expectations and responsibilities of an officer. He served on ten
ships—*Lively* 38, *Unité* 36, *Leviathan* 74, *Conqueror* 74, *Impétueux* 74,
Dublin 74, *Venerable* 74, *Bulwark* 74, *Tonnant* 80, and *Vengeur* 74—before
his May 1815 promotion to lieutenant. This early service allowed Robert
little chance to distinguish himself, but provided lively fodder for his
memoir.[10]

---

8 Population records for 1792 set the population of Musselburgh at 4,015, within a total
   parish population of 5,392. For additional historical data, see Peter McNeill,
   Prestonpans and Vicinity: Historical, Ecclesiastical and Traditional (1902; Prestonpans
   Historical Society, 2004), http://www.prestoungrange.org/prestonpans/html/press/
   vicinity/252.htm; *Inveresk (Midlothian): Records, Sources, and Information about the
   Parish of Inveresk and the Burgh of Musselburgh*, http://www.ancestor.abel.co.uk/
   Inveresk.htm; and "Musselburgh: East Lothian," *The Gazetteer for Scotland*, http://
   www.geo.ed.ac.uk/scotgaz/towns/townfirst280.html.

9 Assorted family papers and genealogical records are in the possession of George
   Aitchison's great-great-granddaughter, Helen Mound, Worcestershire, UK; additional
   genealogical data retrieved from General Register Office for Scotland, *Scotlandspeople*,
   http://www.scotlandspeople.gov.uk/. W. F. K. Thompson discusses the Aitchison family in his introduction to John Aitchison's *An Ensign in the Peninsular War*; David
   Aitchison's career is discussed by Gavin White, "Glasgow," *The Scottish Episcopal
   Church: A New History*, http://www.episcopalhistory.org.uk/07glasgow.html and
   Michael Moss, "Learning and Beliefs: Episcopalians," *The Glasgow Story*, http://the
   glasgowstory.com/story.php?id=TGSCC04.

10 William R. O'Byrne, ed., *A Naval Biographical Dictionary: Comprising the Life and
   Services of Every Living Officer in Her Majesty's Navy, from the Rank of Admiral of the
   Fleet to that of Lieutenant, Inclusive* (London, 1849), 7; Michael Lewis, *A Social History
   of the Navy, 1793-1815* (London, 1960), 88-90.

The early portions of Aitchison's memoir describe the life of a young naval officer sailing in the English Channel, serving on French blockading duty in the Mediterranean, and chasing American privateers along the New England coast. He describes his role in the French siege of Cadiz, Spain; the British blockade of Toulon, France; and the August 1810 shipwreck of HMS *Lively*, a frigate on which he was then serving. The juxtaposition of monumental and trivial events is instructive—military life unfolds this way before it is condensed and edited for the history books.

At times, Aitchison's manuscript reads more like a datebook than a memoir—heavy on data, light on reflection. But as we follow Aitchison from post to post, we gain insight into the rhythms of naval life and the relationships that develop among ship's personnel. Aitchison inserts pointed commentary about his companions, high and low. We learn of his respect for the "very gruff" Captain David Milne; his lack of confidence in Lieutenant Henry Slade, a "slow old chap"; his sympathy for "poor Dick" Baird, who suffers from consumption; his concern for John O'Reilly, whose promotion to lieutenant is too long delayed; and his affinity for Captain James Gordon, whom Aitchison finds "full of fun." On several occasions Aitchison admits to a fear of the unknown: the "bitter moment," shortly after his enlistment, when he feels abandoned by his father and later, in Louisiana, when he is a "little afraid that some stray alligators . . . might make a meal of" him. He feels embarrassment when, as a thirteen-year-old midshipman, his small-boat oarsmen place him in a wheelbarrow and roll him around the streets. As his memoir progresses, Aitchison finds a new confidence—and a new "family." A telling episode takes place in 1810, when his brother George visits him on the Island of Malta; grateful as he is for the visit, Aitchison realizes that he would rather "get back . . . and join [his] messmates."

The memoir moves at a brisk pace. At only one point does Aitchison pause and allow past, present, and future to overlap. "I have no business to attempt to describe what the army did, and I possibly would make many mistakes," he comments, apropos of the Battle of New Orleans. "All that I wish is, to acquaint my children, what part I acted in these juvenile days." This rare authorial intrusion signals that Aitchison attached great importance to this chapter of his life. He refuses to sugar-coat his account of the New Orleans campaign—but he does slow the pace of his narrative to chronicle the unfolding events. Aitchison remembered that in November 1814, "there was now no doubt of our going to make an attack on New Orleans." The British expedition "swelled into a large squadron" and anchored off the coast of the Chandeleur Islands. Before any land assault could begin, the American naval force on Lake Borgne, commanded by Lieutenant Thomas ap Catesby Jones, would have to be eliminated. Aitchison hoped to join the attack force but only lieutenants or passed midshipmen were selected to command the assault boats; since he had not yet passed his examination, Aitchison remained behind. This exclusion probably saved his life. British casualties during the sea-borne attack were significant, and Aitchison's companion "Rob" Uniacke died from wounds suffered during the battle. But Aitchison did find a way to participate, if not in a direct combat role. He secured command of Admiral Sir Edward Codrington's gig, which carried the admiral's "valet and shoe brushes." His assertiveness allowed him to venture to the front of the British lines and to see the battle firsthand—an experience that became the highlight of his memoir.[11]

Aitchison spent forty more years slowly and methodically climbing the navy's seniority ladder. He passed his lieutenant's exam just days after the Battle of New Orleans. But then his career stalled. From the time he won promotion to commander in 1819 until his promotion to captain in 1827, he walked the quarterdeck of only one ship. Even more exasperating, he never commanded a single ship after being promoted to captain. Instead he spent the remainder of his career on half pay, retiring as a captain in 1849 and earning a post-retirement promotion to rear admiral in 1854. Despite the promotions—and the recognition they brought from fellow officers, family, and friends—nothing in Aitchison's career ever compared to the professional excitement he experienced in the years between 1814 and 1816.

Aitchison may have conceived of his memoir as a unique personal document, a literary bequest to his children—but it can also be seen as a

---

11 For a discussion of the Battle of Lake Borgne, see Gene A. Smith, *Thomas ap Catesby Jones: Commodore of Manifest Destiny* (Annapolis, 2000), 27-29.

representative work of British nationalism. The memoir belongs to a genre, "the young subaltern abroad," that became increasingly popular during the mid-nineteenth century. More than one hundred military memoirs from the period were published before 1912, most of them reminiscences of the Napoleonic Wars in Europe. Victories in Europe, under the heroic command of the Duke of Wellington and Admiral Horatio Nelson, held appeal for British readers. Defeat in North America did not. While American authors—and Frenchmen such as Arsène Lacarrière Latour—celebrated the outcome of the Battle of New Orleans and praised General Andrew Jackson, British authors largely looked elsewhere.[12]

Those few British officers who discussed the North American campaigns did so, most often, in an effort to salvage their own reputations. One such work appeared in 1815, shortly after the war's end. Thomas Mullins, who had been prosecuted for failing to bring forward the ladders and fascines needed to cross the American ditches at Chalmette, published an account of his court-martial. Although Mullins mounted a spirited defense, the testimony gained little notice outside army circles. The first major autobiographical examination of the war came from George Robert Gleig (1796-1888), who later became the chaplain-general of the British army. In 1821 he published an account of the British army at Washington and New Orleans, which offered a succinct explanation of British and American failures and successes, descriptions of the regions in which fighting occurred, and suggestions for how the British might have defeated the Americans. Gleig's biased perspective

---

12 A comprehensive bibliographic record can be found in Charles Oman's *Wellington's Army, 1809-1814* (London, 1913). The market for nineteenth-century military memoirs remains strong to this day; historians continue to resurrect—and readers continue to respond to—long-buried manuscripts, like Arsène Lacarrière Latour's *Historical Memoir of the War in West Florida and Louisiana in 1814-15*, ed. Gene A. Smith (Gainesville, 1999). Of the posthumously published British accounts of North American campaigns, several of the most interesting describe events along the Canadian frontier: William Dunlop's *Recollections of the American War, 1812-14* (Toronto, 1905); Mohawk chief John Norton's *Journal*, ed. Carl F. Klinck and James J. Talman (Toronto, 1970); and *Merry Hearts Make Light Days: The War of 1812 Journal of Lieutenant John Le Couteur, 104th Foot*, ed. Donald E. Graves (Ottawa, 1993).

stimulated sales and prompted additional printings in Britain but, not surprisingly, the book sold poorly in the United States. A decade later Norman P. Pringle, John Henry Cooke, and Benson E. Hill published similar descriptions of the British war in North America. Not surprisingly, none found many readers in the patriotic American market of the Jacksonian era.[13]

As the nineteenth century bled into the twentieth, perspectives on the War of 1812 started to lose their partisan edge. Interest in the war, and in its decisive battle, ran particularly strong in New Orleans. In 1943, General L. Kemper Williams began assembling a vast collection of manuscripts, books, pamphlets, maps, drawings, and paintings focusing on the Battle of New Orleans—materials that eventually would form the heart of The Historic New Orleans Collection. In 1952, General Williams acquired the Aitchison memoir from dealer Albert Lieutaud. The manuscript stands as a centerpiece of The Collection; its publication should be a welcome event for readers on both sides of the Atlantic. Aitchison's insights into military life—and his descriptions of the flora and fauna of nineteenth-century Louisiana, New England, Canada, Cuba, and Bermuda—make him our British eyewitness at an important turning point in American history.

---

13 Turnaround time for the publication of war narratives was often quick. Manuscripts relating to the Battle of New Orleans—such as Thomas Mullins's account of his court-martial—appeared as early as 1815, as did the earliest book-length accounts of the War of 1812. Notable early studies include Gideon M. Davison and Samuel Williams, *Sketches of the War, between the United States and the British Isles . . .* (Rutland, VT, 1815) and William James, *A Full and Correct Account of the Military Occurrences of the Late War between Great Britain and the United States of America . . .* (London, 1818).

Brussels 1857
R A, PROCEEDINGS FROM THE TIME HE ENTERED THE NAVY

CHAPTER I

Apprenticeship at Sea, 1808–1813

ON THE 31 DECEMBER 1808, being then in the 13th year of my age I was taken on board the *Ardent*[1] of 64 guns,[2] the Flagship at Leith Roads by my kind friend Captain David Milne,[3] the Father of the present Rear Admiral Alexander Milne, and on that day was entered as a volunteer of the first class, (afterwards to become a midshipman). My friend was in command of the Sea Fencibles[4] at the time, but we had a man of war boat to take us on board, and bring us ashore. This ceremony being over, my uniform made, & of which I was not a little proud, I was sent back to school on 4 months leave, and I saw nothing more of the *Ardent*.

About the month of April I was approached to join the *Lively*,[5] a 38-gun Frigate on the Lisbon Station, and commanded by Captain George Mackinley,[6] a most excellent man, and a good officer.

---

1 The 64-gun HMS *Ardent*, launched in 1783, was then the flagship of the British Squadron at Leith Roads—the naval station just to the northeast of Edinburgh, Scotland. Leith Roads is presently a part of Edinburgh. During the war with the United States, the frigate served as a prison ship on the North American station.

2 When referring to ships of the Royal Navy, Aitchison often follows the convention of the time—to give the name of the vessel followed by a number indicating the number of guns the vessel carries. First-rate ships-of-the-line generally carried more than 100 guns on three decks, while second-rate ships carried from 90 to 98 guns on three decks. Third-rate, or medium-sized ships, had anywhere from 64 to 84 guns on two decks, while fourth-rate ships, considered large frigates, generally carried 50 to 54 guns. Fifth-rate ships, or medium frigates, generally carried 44 guns, while sixth-rate ships, or small frigates, carried 30 to 40 guns. British sloops generally carried from 18 to 30 guns, while smaller brig-sloops carried 12 to 18 guns on single decks.

3 David Milne from Edinburgh joined the navy in May 1779 and during the American War for Independence saw action in the second relief of Gibraltar and in the Caribbean. From 1783 to 1793, he worked in the East India merchant trade. Milne reentered the service with the renewed war against France and quickly distinguished himself—he was promoted to lieutenant in January 1794, to commander in April 1795, and to captain in October 1795. Over the next several years he sailed in the Caribbean and along the coasts of France and Africa, where in August 1800 he encountered and defeated the French frigate *Vengeance*. He later served on the Lisbon and North American stations.

4 Sea Fencibles were the coastal militia responsible for protecting the coast of Britain from invasion.

5 HMS *Lively*, a 38-gun small frigate constructed at the Chatham Dockyard in 1804, had served on the Lisbon station and in the Mediterranean during the war with France.

6 George Mackinley (more often spelled M'kinley) joined the navy in August 1773 as a captain's servant; he was promoted to lieutenant in January 1782, to commander in May 1798, and to captain in October 1801.

Sir David Milne from Edward Pelham Brenton, The Naval History of Great Britain *(London, 1837). The patronage of Milne, a fellow Scot, greatly advanced Aitchison's career, affording him opportunities unavailable to many of his peers.*

Accordingly I was shipped off in a Leith smack[7] with my brother George, to look after me, my Father having gone to London by land. We had a foul wind, nearly the whole way, and blowing strong as I thought, as I was very sick, as well as George. At the end of Ten long days & nights, we arrived in the Thames, and I remember a poor little child on board, who I suppose was very thirsty, seizing hold of a bottle of whiskey and drank enough to kill her very soon.

We stayed in London about a week, and then departed for Portsmouth,[8] my Father George & me Posting all the way, and sleeping one night on the road, at Liphook. Arriving at Portsmouth, we took up our quarters at the "Crown," a large Hotel in the High Street, a little below the "George." It has been shut up ever since the peace of 1816. My Father went across to the Admiral's office, to present a letter, which I brought to him, of introduction, from somebody or other. The Admiral was old Sir Roger Curtis,[9] who received my Father very courteously, and instructed him what to do with me. Now came the bitter moment of parting, with everyone who seemed to care one farthing about me, but off I went, bid good bye to my Father & George, and was sent on board the *Royal William*,[10] or *Royal Billy* as she was familiarly called, the guard ship at Spithead,[11] and put under the charge of a fine old fellow, Mr. Cumming,[12] the First Lieutenant, who took me to the wardroom,[13] where I messed (paying my keep) all the time I was on the ship, and I had also a Cot, hung up for me in one of the wardroom cabins, so I was kept out

---

7 A smack was a small sailing vessel rigged as a hoy (single masted with a fore-and-aft sail). Smacks were generally used for general harbor duties or as associates to larger vessels.

8 Portsmouth, a seaport and naval depot in Hampshire facing the English Channel, was the site of the most important Royal Naval station of the eighteenth and nineteenth centuries; it remains an important naval facility.

9 Roger Curtis from Downton in Wiltshire entered the navy in 1762. He served off the coasts of Africa and Newfoundland before being promoted to lieutenant in 1771. At the beginning of the American War for Independence, Curtis served on the North American station, where he remained until 1778. Winning recognition for his service in the Mediterranean and for his defense of Gibraltar, Curtis was knighted and promoted to captain. He became a rear admiral in July 1794, a baronet the following September, and was promoted to admiral in April 1804. Curtis took command of the Portsmouth naval yard in January 1809 and served as president of the August 1809 court-martial that tried and acquitted Lord Gambier in his dispute with Sir Thomas Cochrane. He died in November 1816.

10 HMS *Royal William* was originally the 100-gun ship-of-the-line commissioned in 1670 as *The Prince*. Renamed in 1692 and rebuilt in 1719, the ship served on active duty until 1790. During the wars with France, the vessel functioned as a guard ship for Portsmouth harbor until it was broken up in August 1813.

11 Spithead was the roadstead for the British fleet on the southern coast of England; it lay between Portsmouth and the northeast coast of the Isle of Wight.

12 The Mr. Cumming to whom Aitchison refers may have been James Cumming, who was promoted to lieutenant in December 1805.

13 The wardroom served as the living quarters in which commissioned officers in the Royal Navy ate their meals, slept, and spent their spare time. The ship's commanding officer had separate, private quarters.

of the company of a great many raffish fellows in the Midshipmen's[14] berth. One First Lieutenant always wore a Cocked hat, the Uniform hat was then a very plain affair, no epaulettes, and the edge of the coat had a white cord on it. Every morning at 8 o'clock, we used to cross top gallant yards,[15] a ceremony followed by all the men-of-war, which happened to be at Spithead, the old Billy had only Jury masts.[16] I employed my time, which hung heavy, in running up & down the rigging, & paddling about in the boats, hanging alongside. We had no schoolmaster, so that all that I had learned, was beginning to ooze out of me. I think I must have been here a month, when I was ordered on board the *Jasper*, a little 10-gun brig[17] commanded by Captain Daniel,[18] to take a passage to Lisbon to join the *Lively*. I felt somewhat uncomfortable on board this Brig, but I bore well up, and first tasted grog[19] here, which I thought most capital stuff, but I am happy to say, I never indulged in it afterwards, or ever thought so highly of it, as I did at that first taste. I don't know why we did not sail immediately but it was fortunate for me we did not, as some one told me that the *Lively* had left for England, so I sent to my friend Mr. Cumming, and told him what I had heard, & he had me on board the *R[oya]l William* again, and a few days afterwards, to my great joy, the

14 Naval midshipmen were young gentlemen who were students in training for commissions as officers in the Royal Navy. Starting as volunteers or by appointment from the first lord of the Admiralty, midshipmen automatically became rated after three years of service; after six years they took an examination for promotion to the rank of lieutenant. In the meantime, these potential officers had the privilege of walking the quarterdeck.

15 Topgallant yards or spars held the topgallant sails, which were usually the uppermost sails of a square-rigged, three-sail mast.

16 Jury masts were temporary or makeshift masts used in the case of storm or battle damage.

17 The term "brig" refers to a two-masted vessel with a square rig on both fore and main masts. Brigs were traditionally used for short or coastal voyages.

18 William Westcott Daniel, commander of the 10-gun *Jasper*, became a lieutenant in October 1798 and was promoted to commander in December 1805. Aitchison refers to Daniel as "captain," which is an honorary title given to a vessel's senior officer, regardless of his official rank; Daniel was not promoted to captain until December 1813.

19 Although grog is a slang expression for any alcoholic beverage mixed with water, the British navy generally used rum in the mixture.

Lively arrived, so on board I went, and soon got settled among a very nice set of fellows as messmates. A short time before this, by the bye, I saw that magnificent expedition sail for Flushing. No steamers in those days all depended on sails.

(1809)

THE *LIVELY* WAS ORDERED to the Downs,[20] to take the Flag of Sir George Campbell[21] the Admiral there, and there we lay a month and a very stupid time it was, and I never quitted the ship. At length we were ordered back to Portsmouth, and we sailed somewhere about July. We had a foul wind but one morning at Daylight we gave chase to a large French lugger[22] Privateer, which had been hovering near us in the night, with all her sails down, so we did not see her. The chase was to me, my entry, a very exciting one. She was dead to leeward,[23] so we ran down with studding sails[24] both sides, but could not gain upon her. Unfortunately for the French man, two more men-of-war hove in sight, & gave chase the *Isis*[25] & *Plover*.[26] One appeared on her starboard[27] beam, the other on her

---

20 The Downs is a roadstead some nine miles long and six miles wide along the southeast coast of Kent, between North and South Foreland in the English Channel. The site affords an excellent anchorage and is protected by the Goodwin Sands, a natural breakwater.

21 Admiral George Campbell was commanding at the Downs in 1809 in the flagship *Princess of Orange*. At the time that Aitchison encountered Campbell in 1809, he was the Rear Admiral of the Red—a position he had held since its creation in November 1805. The grade of Admiral of the Red was second only to that of Admiral of the Fleet; a Rear Admiral of the Red was the eighth ranking officer of the navy.

22 A lugger is a small vessel rigged with a four-sided sail of unequal vertical dimensions.

23 Leeward means downwind.

24 Studding sails were extra sails set only in fine weather outside the square sails of a ship. They were set by extending the yards with booms. Aitchison's account indicates that the two vessels, once engaged, were sailing with or running before the wind.

25 HMS *Isis*, a 50-gun frigate constructed in 1774 at Henniker on the River Medway, served on blockade duty during the wars against France. The ship was broken up in September 1810, shortly after Aitchison encountered the vessel.

26 HMS *Plover*, an 18-gun sloop, was launched in April 1796 at Betts, Mistleyhorn. The sloop spent most of her short career on blockade duty off the coast of France and was decommissioned and sold in March 1819.

27 Starboard means to the right.

Map of England and Scotland by Tracy Smith

Larboard[28] (or Port beam now designated) so there was little chance for him. At length the *Plover* (I believe it was) got within range of him, and it was not until he was fired into, his main mast crippled and the man at the helm, the only one on deck, was wounded that she rounded to. She proved to be the "*Aurore*," a new privateer lugger, pierced for 14 guns, & 70 men on board all of whom were brought on board the *Lively*, and we sent a midshipman & men (we being [the] Commodore) on board her, who took her into Dover.[29] The French Privateers were so numerous in the channel at this time, that one of them had the audacity to try & recapture the *Aurore*, when running into Dover harbour, and while we were lying in Dungeness Bay,[30] wind bound, on our passage round, several of them came almost within gunshot of us. Our Captain signaled the *Podargus*[31] Brig to slip her cable and chase, but they were too nimble for her and soon were far beyond her reach. These were events of every day occurrence and although our cruizers were very numerous, still these Privateers picked up a great many of our merchant vessels.[32]

We reached Portsmouth at last, after beating about the channel for three weeks, and we were ordered into the Harbour to be docked, the ship

---

28 Larboard or port means to the left.

29 Dover was a port and naval base some sixty miles east-southeast of London. Since the port was the most important gateway to the European continent, it was well protected by the navy.

30 Dungeness Bay was the entry to the port of Dover.

31 HMS *Podargus*, a 14-gun brig-sloop launched in May 1808, served on dockyard and harbor duty at Portsmouth until she was sold in August 1833.

32 Cruising against privateers was one of the most exciting and lucrative duties for sailors and officers. Once a privateer had been captured, the victorious commanding officer manned it with a prize crew, or men spared from his ship; the prize crew would take the vessel to a friendly port where, depending on circumstances, it would be adjudicated and condemned as a prize of war. Once condemned, the vessel and its contents were sold and the proceeds awarded to the officers and crew who had made the capture. During the post-1808 period, a victorious captain received a ²⁄₈ share of the total proceeds; the higher ranking commissioned or warrant officers—including marine and army captains, navy lieutenants, sailing masters, and ships' surgeons—shared ¹⁄₈ of the proceeds; a third group comprising marine and army lieutenants, admirals' secretaries, principal warrant officers, masters' mates, and chaplains also shared a ¹⁄₈ share; and the remaining half of the profits was distributed according to rank among midshipmen, inferior warrant officers, warrant officers' mates, marine sergeants, able and ordinary seamen, landmen and servants, and volunteers and boys. Prizes could also be won by capturing a commissioned vessel from an enemy's navy and selling it to one's own government.

having been ashore on a rock in Vigo bay,[33] and knocked a large piece off her forefoot & false keel.[34]

We were obliged to remain nearly the whole winter, before a Dock was vacant, and a very idle time this was for we youngsters, without a schoolmaster on board. But I was sent ashore every day, with two other mids[hipmen] to a Monsieur Delarue, at Portsm[outh], to have French lessons, and my duties as a young gentleman of 13, were to take the Daily Progress[35] to the Admiral's office, and go on shore at midnight to wait at Stoney Steps farport, for Mr. F. N.[36] the First Lieutenant, who used to attend the Tea & evening parties. I had some difficulty in keeping my boats men together occasionally, and once when I suppose they were a little unsteady they took a fancy to wheel me, their officer, about the High Street, in a wheelbarrow. Very wrong no doubt, but still I kept them together at the expense of my own dignity.

(1810)

WE HAD A RUSSIAN SQUADRON in the harbour all the winter, 74s with their lower yards & topmasts struck, detained for some purpose or other. The crews were stout looking fellows.

We fitted out in the Spring with a fine ship's company, & the *Lively* looked a perfect Man-of-War. We were ordered to Spithead, and to collect a convoy for Spain & Portugal. After due time we sailed but were obliged to anchor soon again in Weymouth bay,[37] the wind fouling.

We dropped our convoy at Lisbon and went on to Cadiz, which place the French were beseiging at the time, so something exciting was

---

33 Vigo Bay is an inlet on the Atlantic Ocean in northwestern Spain, some seventeen miles south by west of Pontevedra.

34 The forefoot is the part of the keel that curves up to meet the stem, or the place at which the stem joins the keel of a ship. A false keel is an extension to the hull of the ship, usually attached to deepen the vessel's draft so that it has better sailing qualities.

35 The daily progress reports, generally compiled by the ship's first lieutenant or executive officer, were reports indicating the status of a ship.

36 It is possible that F. N. was Lieutenant Sir Frederick William Erskine Nicolson who was stationed at Portsmouth at this time.

37 Weymouth Bay is located on the southern coast of England, some fifty-three miles west-southwest of Southampton.

always going on. I rode out with some other youngsters to the Dockyard three miles from Cadiz & passed the fire from the French batteries, but nothing touched us. We saw a good many poor Spaniards lying dead on the beach, &c.

We returned to England, having left General Ferguson[38] at Cadiz. We were again, after a short stay at Spithead, ordered to hoist Sir Charles Cotton's[39] Flag & convey him to the Mediterranean to relieve Lord Collingwood.[40]

Before we reached Cadiz, we fell in with a ship, taking home the body of Lord Collingwood, who died at his post in the Mediterranean, quite worn out in the service. When we arrived at Cadiz, Sir Charles

---

38 Ronald Craufurd Ferguson from Edinburgh entered the army as an ensign in April 1790. Promoted to lieutenant in January 1791, he traveled to Berlin to study the Prussian military system. At the beginning of the French war in 1793, Ferguson was dispatched to Flanders where he served for the duration of the campaign. He served in India, Europe, and Africa before winning promotion to major general in April 1808. In 1810, when Aitchison encountered Ferguson, he had just been appointed second in command of the army in Cadiz, Spain, but illness soon forced him to return to England. He later served in Holland and in the House of Commons, before dying in April 1841.

39 Charles Cotton from London was educated at Westminster and was a member of Lincoln's Inn. He joined the navy in 1772 and became a lieutenant in April 1777 while on the North American station under Lord Richard Howe. Promoted to commander in 1779, he served in the Caribbean until the end of the war. Cotton served in the English Channel after the 1793 outbreak of war with France; he became a captain in February 1797 and a vice admiral in April 1802. By the time Aitchison encountered Cotton, he had been promoted to admiral (December 1808) and appointed to replace Lord Collingwood as commander of the Mediterranean squadron. After being recalled to command the Channel Fleet in May 1811, Cotton died suddenly in February 1812.

40 Cuthbert Collingwood from Newcastle-on-Tyne entered the navy in 1761 at age eleven. He served on the North American station during the American War for Independence, winning promotion to lieutenant in June 1775, and in the Caribbean, becoming a commander in June 1779. It was while serving aboard the *Lowestoft* in the Caribbean that he became associated with Horatio Nelson. After the 1793 outbreak of war with France, Collingwood served in the Mediterranean and again made contact with Nelson. After attaining the rank of rear admiral in February 1799, Collingwood served as Nelson's second in command at the Battle of Trafalgar on October 21, 1805. Nelson died during the engagement, and Collingwood succeeded him as commander, winning much of the glory for the British victory. Collingwood became ill while serving in the Mediterranean in February 1810 and was ordered home at once. He died on March 7.

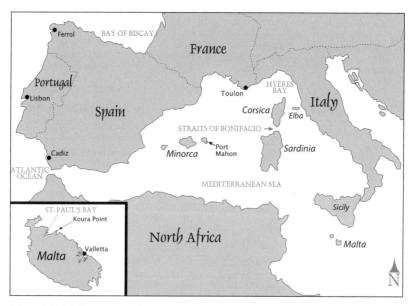

Map of the Mediterranean with inset of Malta by Tracy Smith

Cotton transferred his Flag to the "*San Joseph.*"[41] We hoisted the Flag of Rear Admiral Boyle,[42] and sailed with a convoy to Malta. We had a General Cockburn[43] on board also as a passenger for Sicily. We had a tedious passage to Malta, but at length on the 9th of Aug. we were off the Island, in beautiful weather, and hove to off St. Paul's Bay, intending to run into Valetta harbour in the morning, but alas, it was otherwise ordained. *(1810 Aug)* About 12:30 midnight, the ship being under 3 topsails and the main topsail to the mast, <u>head in shore</u>. The look out man reported to the officer of the watch, Mr. Augustus Berkeley, that he saw breakers on the lee (larboard) bow. This was hardly noticed, but on seeing the fact himself, he made an effort to get the ship's head off shore.[44] He made a noise, which brought poor Captain Mackinley on deck. We hauled the spanker[45] out to bring her round, filled the main topsail, put the helm hard a lee which was a turn and a half a lee before, then hauled the main topsail, which was not of the slightest use, and the ship payed off and struck on the rocks of Coura point.[46] The wind at the time was quite

---

41 HMS *San Joseph* (*St. Josef*) was a 114-gun Spanish ship-of-the-line captured by the British in February 1797 at Cape St. Vincent in the Caribbean. The ship served as an active component of the British fleet until 1837 when it was converted to a gunnery training ship; the *San Joseph* was broken up in May 1849 at Devonport.

42 Aitchison is correct in his recollection that Courtenay Boyle took command of the Mediterranean squadron in the summer of 1810 but incorrect in his attribution of rank: Boyle was but a captain at the time. Nonetheless, as commander of the convoy, Boyle would still be permitted to raise his flag. Boyle had been promoted to lieutenant in 1790 and won promotion to commander in 1795 because he had taken a considerable number of prizes. His promotion to captain in late June 1797 occurred because he had kept his crew under control during the mutinous spring of 1797 (which saw revolts at Spithead and the Nore). From 1803 to 1804 Boyle commanded one of Nelson's patrolling frigates off Toulon, gaining the attention of the admiral after several cutting-out actions. Boyle had little active employment after 1805; the command that Aitchison recalled was but convoy duty, transporting troops to Sicily. Boyle later served as the commander at Sheerness and a commissioner of the Navy Board before ultimately reaching the rank of Vice Admiral of the Red in November 1841.

43 George Cockburn, born in Dublin, entered the army in May 1781. He served at Gibraltar during the siege and on recruiting duty in Dublin, before going abroad to study the military establishments of Prussia, Austria, France, and Spain. After being promoted to major general in 1803, Cockburn was appointed to command a division of the army of occupation in Sicily in April 1810; he remained in command until November 1810, when he gained promotion to lieutenant general. When Cockburn died in August 1847, he was the fourth ranking general of the army. A different George Cockburn (1772-1853) served as rear admiral in the Royal Navy and colonel in the Royal Marines during the War of 1812. He assisted General Robert Ross in the burning of public buildings in Washington, D.C. This Cockburn rose to Admiral of the Fleet in 1815 and carried Napoleon to exile on the island of St. Helena.

44 The *Lively* was sailing from St. Paul's Bay, a large inlet on the northeastern side of the Island of Malta, toward Valetta (often spelled Valletta) harbor, further down the coast to the southeast. One of Britain's strongest naval bases outside of England, Valletta was a frequent rendezvous point for the Mediterranean fleet. But the *Lively* never made it out of St. Paul's Bay. The ship ran aground on a lee shore—a perilous situation that occurs when a ship is hemmed too close to shore by a wind blowing off the sea, leaving the crew no room to maneuver, or "claw off." Unless multiple anchors can be dropped in a firm seabed, securing the ship until the winds change, destruction is practically inevitable.

45 A spanker is an additional sail hoisted on the mizenmast (third, aft-most mast) of a square-rigged sailing ship that permits the vessel to take advantage of a following wind.

46 Koura Point juts into the Mediterranean from the easternmost reaches of St. Paul's Bay.

light. We had Royal yards across,[47] all was now confusion to get the boats out. We were very neat about the rigging, but not what a practical seaman would call in good handy working order. They could not get at the Yard Tackles. They were struck away under hawsers[48] & lumber in the Orlop,[49] and by the time we got them, and hooked, it began to blow & so hard, that one of the quarter boats, which had been sent out with a kedge anchor, was obliged to drop the anchor & run for shelter into St. Paul's Bay. The ship began to bump and then the rudder was knocked away, and then it blew a gale of wind with the sea breaking over us, and the ship nearly on her beam ends, the wind right on the shore. We burned blue lights & fired guns to warn the convoy, not one of which was lost.

The masts were now to be cut away, which was soon done by cutting away the weather lanyards[50] of the lower rigging, and it was beautiful to see these immense spars fall one after the other without a human being hurt. The Admiral & General with the staff were landed, and seeing all efforts to save the ship of no avail, the ship's company was ordered ashore, by walking along the foremast which reached the shore, but the friction of the mast against the side of the ship was so great, that it caught fire, & buckets of water were thrown to keep the fire down. When we reached the rocks, we found the sea making a clean breach right over the reef, so we were obliged to hold on by the rocks, until the sea passed us, and then run for it. As for danger, it never occurred to any of us I believe, that we were in the slightest, but each youngster laughing at the awkwardness of the other, and at the pigs, which had been thrown overboard, and were grunting, and making the best of their way to the shore.

We took up our quarters in Coura Fort, a place full of fleas, garrisoned by the Maltese troops, who left it, to make room for us. Mostly all

---

47 Royal yards held an extra uppermost set of sails on a square rigged ship, which helped vessels in light winds gain additional speed for chasing a foe or outrunning an opponent. A ship needed a large crew to rig these sails.

48 Hawsers are heavy ropes with a circumference of five inches or more.

49 The orlop is the lowest deck level of a ship, directly above the hold.

50 A lanyard is a short piece of rope used for a variety of purposes aboard ship. In this instance lanyards on the ship's weather side–facing the wind–were passed through deadeye rings to keep the lower riggings taut.

our clothes were lost and stolen by the Maltese peasants, who came down to the wreck in swarms. Here, we lived for two months, trying to recover the ship, but to no purpose. We could not heave her off, and she eventually went to pieces, one of the finest frigates of her day, and it almost broke the heart of the Captain. I lost all my clothes, but as good luck would have it, one morning I was sitting in my Embrasure[51] which was our dwelling place, with simply a tarpaulin thrown over the top to keep the sun off, when poor Hay, one of the Mids[hipmen], who was afterward drowned in command of a 10 gun Brig the "*Delight*" off the Mauritius, came to me, and told me that my brother was sitting at the gate of the Fort, my brother!! Sure it was George, who was on his travels, and hearing on his arrival at Girgenti[52] that the *Lively* was lost, he came across and soon found me out. So he took me to Valetta, rigged me out with new clothes, gave me plenty of iced cream, and iced lemonade, and amused me as well as he could, but I got very tired of it, and longed to get back to the wreck, and join my Messmates. He went on to Sicily, and I to St. Paul's bay, quite happy. There we got plenty of grapes to eat, and bathed half a dozen times a day, going into the sea clothes and all on, which consisted of our shirt & trousers. They soon dried on us, and we became as black as the Maltese, and were generally covered with salt, the water evaporated so quickly. The sea eggs[53] were rather troublesome, and dangerous. If you happened to put your foot on one, the prickles stuck into it and festered. One youngster was obliged to have his great toe cut off.

The ship had knocked large holes in the bottom fore & aft, so if we had hove her off in that state, she would have sunk. Accordingly the lower deck was made water tight, and stanchions[54] fore & aft were placed between that & the main deck, and empty casks were put into the hold, to

---

51 An embrasure is an opening in a wall through which a gun can be fired. Usually the opening is enlarged toward the inner face of the wall, permitting the gun to be traversed. A person could sit in the enlarged opening.

52 Girgenti, located on the northern coast of Sicily some fifty-seven miles south-southeast of Palermo, is now known as Agrigento.

53 Sea eggs, or sea urchins, are spiny echinoid echinoderms of the species *sphaerechinus granularis*.

54 Stanchions are upright structural supports, in this instance placed between the lower and main decks.

assist in floating her. Three tiers of empty casks were likewise lashed on the outside of her bends, to assist in floating her. Six pairs of sheers[55] were raised, and purchases applied to spars, run through the main deck ports, and the falls brought to 4 capstans,[56] shipped on the upper deck. We had also a seaward purchase from a jury topmast, lashed to the stump of the main mast, and on to anchors laid out to seaward. The ship, after one or two failures, was brought upright, and then hove down on the other side, but we could not budge her, and finally saved all the stores we could & abandoned her.

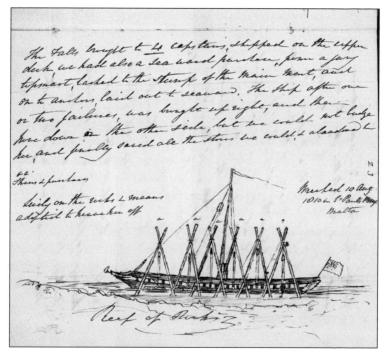

"Lively on the rocks and means adopted to heave her off. Wrecked 10 Aug 1810 in St. Pauls Bay Malta" (from Aitchison memoir)

The *Lively* ship's company were sent round to Valetta, and we were all put on board the *"Trident,"*[57] the guardship, to wait a passage to

Mahon, to be tried by a court martial for the loss of the ship. The officer of the watch at the time she struck and the master were put under arrest. On board this old guardship we had nothing to do, and there I am ashamed to say, I learned to smoke a long Turkish pipe.

After a time, we were transferred to the *Victorious* 74, Captain Talbot,[58] a ship celebrated afterwards for having captured after a sharp action, the *Rivoli*, a French 80.[59] We anchored one night in the Straights of Bonifacio.[60] I went ashore with other youngsters on Sardinia. I remember being much struck with the quantity of Arbutus,[61] growing there & covered with fruit.

The *Victorious* arrived in due time at Minorca, where we found the Fleet lying, a court martial assembled. Captain Mackinley and officers were tried for the loss of the ship; the Captain was acquitted,[62] the Lieutenant of the watch received an admonition, and the master was broke.

---

55 Sheers are temporary structures of two or three spars raised at an angle and lashed together at the point of intersection. They are often used to lift heavy weights on board ship where derricks are not available.

56 A capstan is a cylindrical barrel fitted in larger ships on the forecastle deck that is used for heavy lifting work, particularly working anchors.

57 The 64-gun HMS *Trident*, launched from Plymouth in April 1768, had become a guard ship on the Mediterranean station by the beginning of the nineteenth century. The ship was sold at Malta in July 1816 at the end of the wars with France.

58 John Talbot of Malahide Castle in Dublin entered the navy in 1784. He served with Nelson in the West Indies, making lieutenant in 1790. After cruising in the Mediterranean and capturing a larger French vessel in 1795, Talbot won promotion to commander; he became a captain in August 1796. Talbot's reputation as an aggressive captain won him command of HMS *Victorious* in October 1809.

59 HMS *Victorious*, a 74-gun ship-of-the-line launched in 1784, fought its most famous engagement in February 1812 against the larger *Rivoli*, emerging triumphant in a five-hour battle off the coast of Venice. Afterwards, the *Victorious* returned to England for repairs. During the war with the United States, she served in the West Indies and along the coast of North America.

60 The Straits of Bonifacio are located between the islands of Corsica and Sardinia in the Mediterranean Sea.

61 Arbutus is an evergreen shrub or tree that produces scarlet berries.

62 M'kinley's career was not adversely affected by the *Lively* incident. In 1821 he was appointed superintendent of the Royal Naval Asylum; he reached the rank of rear admiral in July 1830 and vice admiral in November 1841.

We, the Midshipmen, were distributed with different ships. I was sent on board the *Unité*,[63] a noble little Frigate commanded by Patrick Campbell,[64] one of the very best & smartest officers in the service. We were ordered off Toulon, to watch the French Fleet, and had under our orders three other Frigates. The Fleet remained in Mahon harbour[65] during the winter. We reconnoitered the French Fleet in the harbour every day, occasionally they came out, and chased us off, and on one occasion, they very nearly caught us. It was very monotonous work, and we had often during these winter months, very hard gales of wind. We had a little variety one day. Being to the Eastward we observed a convoy in shore. The ship was anchored to keep a battery (which protected this convoy) in check. The boats went under a sharp fire of grape shot[66] from an armed vessel in charge of the convoy, but they succeeded in bringing out one of them, laden with olive oil. The Lieutenant commanding the boats, Crabbe (still poor fellow a Lieutenant)[67] was severely wounded in the groin. I received two dollars for this, my first prize money. We resumed our station off Toulon, and nothing particular occurred until one morn-

---

63 HMS *Unité*, formerly the French *Imperieuse*, was a 40-gun frigate captured by a British squadron in October 1793 off the coast of Spezia, Italy. Renamed in 1803, the ship served in the Mediterranean squadron during the wars with France; she was demoted to harbor duty in 1832 and broken up at Chatham in January 1858.

64 Patrick Campbell from Melfort in Argyllshire became a lieutenant in September 1794, a commander in September 1797, and a captain after his daring capture of a French frigate in July 1800. In 1807 Campbell gained command of the *Unité* and for the next four years sailed in the Adriatic Sea. Known for being an active and energetic officer, he commanded the *Leviathan* in the Mediterranean from 1811 until 1815. Campbell became a rear admiral in July 1830 and a vice admiral in June 1838. He died in October 1841.

65 Mahon harbor, better known as Port Mahon, is a fortified harbor on the southern coast of the Spanish island of Minorca.

66 The term "grapeshot" refers to clusters of grape-sized projectiles fired shotgun style from cannons to sweep enemy decks of seamen, or to damage sails and rigging.

67 William Joseph Crabb entered the Royal Navy in 1801 as a midshipman aboard the *Royal Sovereign*. He won promotion to lieutenant in June 1809 after taking part in the capture of the *Il Roncio*, *Nettuno*, and *Toulie*. Crabbe retired as a lieutenant, as Aitchison noted, yet was promoted to retired commander in July 1851—much like Aitchison, who secured the appointment of retired rear admiral. Crabbe died in 1877.

ing we found the whole French Fleet in chase of us, & to windward of us, with the wind blowing on the land they stupidly came down upon us, with their foretopmast studding sails set. We kept our wind, blowing strong too, so when we saw that we could weather them, "'bout ship," and passed to windward of the whole French Fleet, & out of gunshot.[68]

The winter over, we returned to Mahon, and Captain Campbell was appointed to the *Leviathan* 74 and he took me with him.[69] We did not like the change from an active Frigate to one of the Blockades Fleet, but there was no help for it, and we sailed with the Fleet consisting of only 10 sails of the line to blockade a Fleet I believe pretty nearly double. Sir Edward Pellew afterwards Lord Exmouth[70] was our Commander in Chief. It was a beautiful sight to see our Fleet sail from the narrow entranced harbour of Mahon, with a scant wind. Not a ship got foul of the other, warping up to the weather shore, then smartly making sail, and getting to sea, without an accident. We had no steam to assist us then.

---

68 British seamen often sought the advantage of being upwind of the enemy. This position was called "holding the weather gage"; it gave a captain the option of either bringing his ship into action at a time of his choosing or avoiding action if he faced a larger enemy force.

69 HMS *Leviathan*, a 74-gun ship commissioned in October 1790, served on blockade duty in the Mediterranean during the wars with France. In October 1816 the *Leviathan* was converted to a convict ship and remained as such for thirty years; in October 1846 it became a target ship. The *Leviathan* was sold out of the service in August 1848.

70 Sir Edward Pellew, first Viscount Exmouth, entered the navy in 1770 and soon made voyages to the Falkland Islands and to the Mediterranean. During the American War for Independence he won recognition while serving on Lake Champlain; taken prisoner with General John Burgoyne at Saratoga, Pellew was exchanged and returned to England, where he was promoted to lieutenant. Pellew gained promotion to commander when he damaged and drove ashore the privateer *Stanislaus* in 1780; in 1782 he gained promotion to post rank when he engaged and drove ashore three privateers. After war began between England and France in 1793, Pellew captured the first French frigate in June of that year and was knighted for his service. In May 1799 he quelled a potential mutiny at Bantry Bay and in 1804 received promotion to the rank of rear admiral; he subsequently served in the East Indies and became a vice admiral. In 1810, as commander in chief of the North Sea squadron, he blockaded the enemy's fleet in the Scheldt; the following year Pellew became the commander in chief of the Mediterranean station, where he remained off Toulon until the end of the war.

H.M.S. *Hydra* cutting out ships at Begur Aug 7th 1807.
© *National Maritime Museum, London. Small boats from HMS* Hydra *attempt to seize an enemy ship in the Catalan port of Begur. While on blockade duty in the Mediterranean, Aitchison participated in several cutting-out missions.*

Arriving off Toulon, we stood off & on every day, & looked at the Frenchmen, who came out occasionally to exercise, but they always took care that it should be with a wind, which would enable them to get back. We never could get them within range of our guns.

We had a very interesting chase one morning, and were all at Quarters, in the vain hope that it might bring on a general action. A French Frigate was observed, in the passage between the Island of Poquerolles, one of Hieres,[71] and the main land, evidently intending to run under the protection of the batteries into Toulon. The French Fleet beat out, the British Fleet stood in, and signal was made to the *Franchise*,[72] one of our in shore squadron to chase and cut off the French Frigate, who had bore up to run the gauntlet. Our Frigate wanted "dash." He did not go at him as fast as he might, to the great disgust of we lookers on, and I believe to the Commander in Chief, who made the signal to the *Franchise* to "make more sail" but it was too late. The Frenchman escaped, the French Fleet ran back and we stood off.

For nine long months we cruized off Toulon, watching the French Fleet but they would give us no opportunity of bringing them to action. By way of variety, we came to an anchor in Heires bay and continued there for three weeks. Every morning before daylight we beat to quarters, and kept ready for action, but no alarm of any kind. While we were at anchor here, the French threw up a Battery, on the Island of Poquerolles to molest us in going out, and unluckily it fell calm, just when we got into the passage, and the *Temeraire*[73] lay end on to this battery, and within gunshot. She was hulled several times, and had some casualties among the men, but

---

71 The Hieres or Hyères in the Mediterranean Sea off the southeast coast of Toulon consist of three islands—Port Cros, Ile du Levant, and Porquerolles.

72 HMS *Franchise* was originally a French warship serving along the northern coast of France. The 36-gun frigate—captured in the English Channel by the British navy in May 1803—was transferred to the Mediterranean where it served on blockading duty until it was broken up in November 1815.

73 HMS *Temeraire* was a 98-gun, line-of-battle ship launched from Chatham Dockyard in September 1798. The ship spent most of its career in the Mediterranean before becoming a prison ship in December 1813. In 1820 it was converted to a receiving ship and remained as such until sold in August 1838.

the moment her broadside was brought to bear on the battery, she knocked it to atoms.

(1811)

ABOUT THIS TIME, my early friend Captain David Milne, was appointed to command *L'Impetueux*[74] 78 in the Baltic, and a letter arrived, requesting I might be sent home to join her. I was very glad of this change in many respects, but I was very sorry to quit the *Leviathan*, for there were some good fellows on board her, and the Captain had been always very kind to me. I took a passage home in the *Conqueror*,[75] Captain Fellowes.[76] We arrived at Plymouth, and I was sent round to Portsmouth in the *Diadem*,[77] & found the *Impetueux* there, and there I was fairly settled. We were soon ordered to take the East India men[78] as far as Madeira, and then go to Lisbon.

We arrived at Lisbon after this was performed, and assisted in landing many of the Regiments going into the interior of Portugal, to reinforce

---

74 HMS *L'Impétueux* was originally the French ship *Amerique*. Captured in June 1794 off Ushant at the Battle of the First of June, the 74-gun ship was renamed and served with the British navy until it was broken up in December 1813. Aitchison identifies this vessel as a 78-gun ship; either he was mistaken or, more likely, the ship had taken aboard additional guns.

75 The 74-gun HMS *Conqueror* was constructed in Graham, Harwich, and launched in November 1801. The ship was decommissioned and broken up at Chatham in July 1822.

76 Thomas Fellowes, born in Minorca, served for several years aboard merchant ships of the East India Company before joining the navy in 1797. He sailed in the East and West Indies before being promoted to lieutenant in 1807; Fellowes was promoted to commander for his bravery during an 1809 raid against Guadeloupe. In August 1810 he gained command of British gunboats at Cadiz and held that post until the following June when he returned to England. Aitchison encountered Fellowes after he had been promoted to captain in March 1811; Fellowes was knighted and eventually achieved the rank of rear admiral. He died in July 1847.

77 The 64-gun HMS *Diadem*, launched from Chatham Dockyard in December 1782, became a troopship in May 1798. She continued in that capacity until her decommissioning and dismantling in September 1832.

78 East India men were merchant ships that carried goods between England and the East Indies.

Lord Wellington's[79] army. Among the number were the 42d Highlanders, a fine body of men, who sadly suffered at the storming of Badjoz.[80] We were suddenly ordered out, to try and intercept two French Frigates, expected home. We ran down to Cape Finisterre, then on to Madeira. No tidings, then to Mogadore on the coast of Africa, thinking they might go there for water, but no, they had not been there, so back we went to Lisbon, and found that we must at one time have been within a very short distance of them, for they were cut off by the *Northumberland*,[81] and driven ashore & destroyed somewhere I believe off Ferrol.[82]

Captain Milne was appointed to some ship at home, and Sir George Berkeley[83] hoisted his Flag on board the *Impetueux*, and Captain Milne & followers young John Dewar & myself among the number, took passage home in the *Loire*.[84] This ship was in a bad state of discipline, the cap-

---

79 Arthur Wellesley, first Duke of Wellington (a.k.a. "the Iron Duke"), was the British general who convinced the government to commit to a war in the Iberian Peninsula. Once British troops had been committed, he won fame for driving French armies from Spain. In June 1815 Wellington, commanding a combined British and Prussian force, defeated Napoleon at the Battle of Waterloo in Belgium.

80 The costly and unsuccessful British siege of the frontier fortress of Badajoz, Spain, began in early May 1811 and lasted until the French liberated the city in late June.

81 The 74-gun HMS *Northumberland*, launched in February 1798 from Barnard, Deptford, was stationed in the Mediterranean during the wars against France. Converted to a hulk in February 1827, she remained on the navy list of ships until her destruction in July 1850.

82 Ferrol, or El Ferrol de Caudillo, is an Atlantic harbor on Spain's northwestern coast. Although Spain surrendered Ferrol to the English in 1805, French forces captured and occupied the port from January to June 1809.

83 George Cranfield Berkeley joined the navy in 1766 and for a short time acted as the personal page of Queen Caroline of Denmark. He sailed in the Gulf of St. Lawrence and in the Mediterranean before being promoted to lieutenant in September 1772. Berkeley served in the English Channel and off the coast of Gibraltar during the American War for Independence. After becoming a rear admiral in February 1799, he commanded the Channel Fleet and the Halifax station at the time of the *Chesapeake-Leopard* affair of June 1807. He later served as commander in chief at Lisbon, Portugal, before retiring from active service in May 1812 as an admiral.

84 HMS *Loire*, originally the French ship *La Loire*, had been captured off the coast of Ireland in October 1798. Incorporated into the British fleet, the 40-gun frigate remained on the navy list of ships until April 1818, when she was broken up.

tain quite an old woman. One night we found some of the breechings[85] of the main deck guns cut through, so we were glad to get out of her. On our arrival in England, Captain Milne went to London, & Dewar, a midshipman about my own age, the Captain's steward, Moir, a good sort of man a most capital shot, and "Peter" the captain's black servant, and myself were sent on board the "*Piedmontaise*"[86] to take a passage to Sheerness,[87] to join the *Dublin*,[88] the ship our Captain was said to be appointed to. On our arrival at the Nore,[89] we, viz. Dewar, myself, Moir, black Peter, two pigs and a pointer, were put into the captain's wherry[90] and told to make the best of our way into the harbour, as the ship was going up the Thames.

(1812)

NONE OF US HAD EVER BEEN in Sheerness harbour, but I having arrived at the mature age of 16, and being senior to Dewar, took command of the wherry.   Moir, a good natured jolly fellow, a native of Musselburgh,[91] took a very Fatherly care of Dewar and me, but he knew nothing about a boat, and black Peter did not know much more.   However having a fair wind and not much of it, we got into the mouth of the har-

---

85   Breechings were the ropes used to secure guns to the side of a ship in order to keep the guns from rolling in rough seas and to catch the guns as they recoiled upon firing. A gun fired with cut breechings would leap backwards unchecked, injuring its crew and possibly doing grave damage to the ship.

86   HMS *Piemontaise*—Aitchison inserts an unnecessary "d"—was originally a French ship captured off Ceylon in March 1808. The 38-gun frigate served with the British fleet until she was broken up at Woolwich in January 1813.

87   Sheerness was the English seaport and naval dockyard on the Isle of Sheppey, some thirty-eight miles east of London.

88   The 74-gun HMS *Dublin* was launched from Rotherhithe, near London, in February 1812. Although the ship had a long career, her service was uneventful: she was reduced to 50 guns in December 1826 and in 1845 was relegated to harbor duty, in which capacity she acted until sold in August 1885.

89   The Nore was an anchorage for Royal Navy vessels near the mouth of the Thames and the site of a major mutiny by British sailors in 1797.

90   A wherry is a light rowboat, usually suited for one person.

91   A suburb of Edinburgh, situated at the mouth of the Esk River, Musselburgh was the site of the Aitchison family estate, Drummore.

bour all well, but just then Dewar, who had been sitting very quietly hold-ing on the sheet,[92] while I was steering, took it into his head all at once to wash piggys face by throwing salt water over it. Not being accustomed to this treatment, he jumped smack overboard, and then his brother pig followed his example, so we were obliged to down sails, and pull after them. Moir of course was very angry, "he did know what the Captain would say if these Portuguese pigs were drowned." Dewar laughed & I laughed, & black Peter held his tongue. After a great deal of trouble, and numerous failures, we succeeded in getting the pigs on board again. We found the *Dublin* among the ships in ordinary.[93] She was not com-missioned, and only the warrant officers, and a few Dockyard men on board, but we took up our quarters without beds or provisions either for ourselves or Pigs, but they, the pigs, very soon helped themselves to some cold Pork, the dinners of the Dockyard men. And this was our first diffi-culty. The authorities knew nothing about the *Dublin* being commis-sioned, but we remained on board for orders. We had nothing to do, so we sometimes got into scrapes. Dewar in pulling up a bucket of water found it was too much for him, & he tumbled overboard, but we picked him up all safe.

It appeared that the *Dublin* was not to be our ship, so we went home on leave, and the Pigs were made a present of to my Father. I enjoyed myself very much at home, having been absent three years. After some lit-tle time, Captain Milne was appointed to the *Venerable*[94] 74 at Portsmouth, and Dewar & me, and sundry other young Scotchmen took a passage in a Troop ship from Leith, and joined the *Venerable* at Spithead. She was a fine ship, and a good crew. We were ordered off Cherbourg to watch the French squadron lying there, and after the winter ended, we went into Portsmouth harbour to refit and restow the hold.

---

92 A sheet is a single line used for trimming a sail to the wind; it is connected to the lower corner of the sail.

93 A ship "in ordinary" is a ship that is not in commission but is maintained with a skele-ton crew, permitting it to be recalled to duty at a moment's notice.

94 HMS *Venerable*, a 74-gun ship-of-the-line commissioned in April 1808, spent most of her career at Plymouth on harbor duty; she was broken up in October 1838.

CHAPTER 1

(1813)

BY THE BYE I FORGOT that we had a cruize on the Banks of Newfoundland, and off the Western Islands, but we took nothing. Indeed we saw nothing to take. I landed several times at St. Michaels,[95] where we had lots of oranges & grapes. I was soon promoted to be masters mate, and a very young one I was, but my Captain was always kind to me, although sometimes like a foolish boy I thought otherwise.

We were again to undergo another change in our ship. The *Venerable* was wanted for Admiral Durham's Flag, to go to the West Indies, and we were appointed to the *Bulwark*[96] 74, a very fine ship, and ordered for North America, we being at [manuscript incomplete]. The *Venerable* sailed badly but Captain Milne had re-stowed the ballast according to his own plan and she then sailed very fast. So much so that on her passage to the West Indies with Admiral Durham[97] she captured two French Frigates.

---

95 The St. Michaels that Aitchison is probably referring to is located on St. Michaels Bay, on the eastern coast of Labrador, Canada.
96 The 74-gun HMS *Bulwark*, originally the *Scipio*, was renamed shortly before her launching from Portsmouth in April 1807. She served on the North American station during the War of 1812 before being decommissioned and broken up in September 1826.
97 Philip Charles Henderson Calderwood Durham entered the navy in May 1777 and immediately saw action in the American War for Independence. He sailed with Lord Richard Howe during the relief of Gibraltar in 1783. Durham served in the Mediterranean and along the coast of Africa as a lieutenant and in the West Indies as a commander. After his promotion to captain, Durham sailed off the coast of France and Ireland. He was promoted to rear admiral in July 1810 and soon thereafter commanded a squadron in the North Sea. In December 1813 Durham was sent out as commander in chief of the Leeward Islands station, with his flag in the *Venerable*; he remained there fighting against both French and American privateers until the summer of 1815. Durham was promoted to vice admiral in August 1819 and to admiral in July 1830. He died in April 1845.

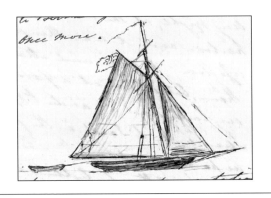

CHAPTER 2

On the North American Station, 1814–1815

(1814)

WE SAILED IN THE *BULWARK* FOR BERMUDA in March 1814 with 2 transports under our convoy, and the *Saturn*, a razeed[1] 74, got up to cope with the large American Frigates. We had a long passage to Bermuda, and bad weather. At length we reached these beautiful islands, covered with the evergreen cedars, all the buildings white. They look quite a Fairy land. The passage into the anchorage is extremely intricate, but the water is so clear, that the rocks and foul ground are easily seen, and the black pilots go entirely by the eye, and often times show most excellent knowledge of seamanship and generally are very smart fellows. Now, I imagine that they have not the same opportunity of showing their skill, as of course steamers are always at hand to tow.

We were ordered off New London[2] and arrived there early in May. We found Sir Thomas Hardy[3] and his squadron there, and we were sent

---

1 The term "razee" refers to a ship-of-the-line that has had its upper deck cut off to lighten its load, subsequently earning a lower gun rating. HMS *Saturn*, originally a 74-gun ship-of-the-line, had her armaments reduced to 58 guns when she was razeed in December 1813. The *Saturn* participated in the 1814 campaigns against the United States and spent her last forty years of service on harbor duty; the ship was broken up at Pembroke Dock in February 1868.

2 New London is a Connecticut seaport situated at the mouth of the Thames River, on the Long Island Sound.

3 Thomas Masterman Hardy from Portisham in Dorset, the only officer of rank present at all three of Lord Horatio Nelson's great victories (Nile, Copenhagen, and Trafalgar), entered the navy in 1781. He sailed in the merchant fleet for a short time and attended school before reentering active service. Hardy won promotion to lieutenant in November 1793, to commander in 1798, and was named a baronet in 1806 for his services to Nelson at Trafalgar. Hardy arrived on the North American station in the spring of 1806 and served there intermittently until the end of the War of 1812. In June 1813, while commanding the *Ramillies* off New London, Hardy captured the sabotaged schooner *Eagle,* which exploded and killed a lieutenant and ten sailors; his cautiousness during the episode spared the lives of many other British sailors. After the war Hardy commanded the South American station, became first sea lord on the Board of Admiralty, and served as governor of the Greenwich Hospital. Hardy was promoted to vice admiral in January 1837; he died two years later in September 1839.

Map of New England and eastern Canada by Tracy Smith. Maine, originally part of the commonwealth of Massachusetts, was admitted to the union in 1820, six years after Aitchison participated in the capture of Castine.

along the coast to Block Island,[4] and our boats captured the first night a little schooner, named the *Experiment*, laden with <u>salt</u> <u>herrings</u>. At 6 am next morning the Captain sent for me and told [me] to go on board her, with five men and take charge of her, as Prize Master. Next day we captured the *Henrietta*, and the *Amelia*, two large coasting sloops,[5] and in a few days afterwards the *Bulwark* sailed for Halifax, with these three prizes. It came on to blow soon after we sailed, with foggy weather. I lost sight of the *Bulwark*, and I thought the best thing I could do was to shape my course for Halifax. I made a good landfall, and had the satisfaction of arriving first at Halifax, and some hours before the *Bulwark*. The Captain seemed much surprised when I made my appearance on board, but he ordered me to give the prize up to the Agents, and rejoin the Ship.

The *Henrietta* was a very nice looking sloop, so the Captain determined to make a Tender[6] of her, and send her into Boston Bay to intercept their coasters. She was armed with a 12-pounder carronade[7] a midships, 10 men, a Lieutenant and myself, as 2nd in command.

We made a bad a start of it, for in beating out of Halifax harbour, we ran the sloop ashore, under York Redoubt, and it was some time before we got her fairly clear. Nothing happened to us in going to Boston bay, and we did not do much after we got there. My commanding officer, a very good man with no enterprise, did not suit me at all. I got him persuaded one night to let me go inshore, in our little whale boat with 4 men & myself, and we lay on our own oars within hail of the American sentries.

---

4 Block Island, located about nine miles off the Rhode Island coast, sits in the Atlantic Ocean at the eastern entrance to Long Island Sound. The body of water between the small island (seven miles long by three and one-half miles wide) and the mainland is Block Island Sound, where Hardy's ships patrolled to block the entrance to Long Island Sound.

5 A sloop-of-war is a single-masted sailing vessel with a fore-and-aft rig and guns on one main deck. It is smaller than a frigate, making it useful in auxiliary roles and in coastal duties.

6 The term "tender" refers to a small vessel attached temporarily to a larger ship for general duties such as collecting mail, delivering fresh vegetables and meat, and delivering seamen ashore.

7 Carronades—named after the maker, Carron Ironworks in Carron, Falkirk, Scotland— were short-barreled, relatively light cannons that fired heavy balls at close range. Because of the lower velocity of the shot, the smashing power was greater and more splinters were thrown to wound enemy sailors. During the late eighteenth and early nineteenth centuries the British navy used carronades as auxiliaries to their main armaments. By the War of 1812, the British had started using carronades as their primary weapon. The rationale seemed sound: the crew-to-cannon ratio was lower for carronades than traditional armaments. A ship carrying carronades could man more weapons with fewer sailors, increasing its broadside strength and gun rating. But the strategy backfired, as the British suffered several humiliating defeats by American ships that carried longer-range guns.

I heard one hail a long low boat creeping close into the land. He did not see us, so on coming up to us, we jumped on board, told the two unfortunate fellows to hold their tongues, which they did, being in a pretty considerable fright. I left two men in her, and then her consort came up, and I took possession of her and pulled to sea and joined the Tender, with my two prizes at daylight. They were long low market boats, full of all sorts of things. We put the cargoes with the Tender and gave the crews back their boats. I got a fresh crew and started on another trip. I was not to successful, but I had a very pretty little chase after another, blazed away at her with my musket, over my crew's heads, but he escaped by running into the surf, and on the beach.

One night I was to have gone in with this same little boat to cut out a schooner[8] under a battery at Marblehead,[9] but it was lucky for me that it came on to blow, & we could not leave the sloop. We should probably have been <u>eaten up</u>.

Slade,[10] my Lieutenant, went on board the *Bulwark* to dine with the Captain one day, and a thick fog came on, and I lost sight of her, so I stood inshore, in quest of adventures, and the next morning at daylight I saw a large rakish looking schooner to leeward beating up a chase of <u>me</u>. I was quite sure he was a Yankee Privateer, and therefore prepared to go to prison, & had the signal books all ready to throw overboard. He soon came up with us, and I thought of giving him a dose of grape shot if he were such, but he showed English colours, and in coming within hail, he hove to, as I did, and he asked what we were. "Tender to the *Bulwark*" and he answered that he was the *Rolla* of Halifax to my great joy, so I went on board him, and found all his men at their guns, 100 I believe, enough to have eaten us up.

I got very tired of this Tender service. If I had had command of

---

8 A schooner is a vessel often rigged with fore-and-aft sails on her two or more masts, permitting it to sail closer to the wind (more directly into the wind's eye). Ideal for trade and fishing, schooners usually carried two gaff sails and a square foretopsail.

9 Marblehead is a Massachusetts town on the Atlantic coast some fifteen miles northeast of Boston.

10 Henry Slade had been a lieutenant since November 1811, serving most of that time aboard the sloop *Philomel*; he was promoted to commander in May 1825.

her, I should have liked it, but old Slade was such a slow old chap, I had made up my mind to ask Captain Milne to take me out of her. However he saw she was of no use, so he put a cargo of captured goods into her and sent her off to Bermuda & I returned to my ship. The *Henrietta* was captured by an American privateer, and carried into New York, where some of our men escaped, and walked to Boston & joined the *Bulwark* once more.

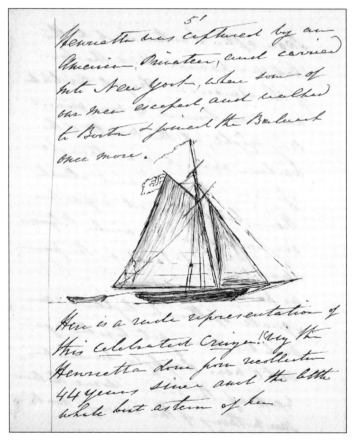

"Here is a rude representation of this _celebrated_ _cruizer_! viz the Henrietta
done from recollection 44 years since and the little whale boat astern of her"
(from Aitchison memoir)

Soon after I returned to the ship, we heard that the boats of the American Frigate *Constitution*[11] were accustomed to row guard every night, at the mouth of the harbour, and it was thought expedient to go in and attack them, but it proved a failure. Our boats went in, under Lieutenant Seymour.[12] I was with Lieutenant Jacobs[13] in the pinnace.[14] We parted company in a heavy squall of thunder lightning & rain, and we never got together again until near daylight. However, we went up the harbour some distance, saw nothing of the enemy's boats but we brought out two Dock Yard Lighters, who took us for their own countrymen, and [we] ransomed them for 100 dollars each.

A day or two after this, we had a most exciting chase after a Briganteen,[15] laden with flour. She was making for Boston, when she caught sight of us, but seeing she had no chance of getting in, she stood boldly out to sea, hoisted her colours, and we after her. She put her head for Nova Scotia. We got almost within range of her when the wind took off. Our shot fell short, and she drew ahead, having thrown a great part of her cargo overboard. We ran her in, close into Cape Sable on the Nova Scotia shore, where we could not follow her, and we were compelled to haul off. Next morning at daylight, we saw our friend again, on the lee bow, and chased again, and were lucky enough to recapture an English

---

11 The USS *Constitution* is one of the six original frigates authorized by the United States Congress in 1794; she is the oldest commissioned warship in the world and is regarded as the most famous ship in the history of the United States Navy. The 44-gun frigate—nicknamed "Old Ironsides" by her sailors because British shots did not penetrate her live-oak timbers—defeated the British frigates *Guerriere* and *Java* in 1812, as well as the frigate *Cyane* and sloop *Levant* in a four-hour battle in 1815. Her initial successes prompted the British Admiralty to prosecute the blockade of the American coastline more vigorously, and as a result the *Constitution* spent much of the war blockaded in the port of Boston.

12 George Alexander Seymour served as a lieutenant aboard HMS *Marlborough*, flagship of Sir George Cockburn, commander in chief of the North American and West Indian stations. Seymour remained a lieutenant until May 1845 and finished his naval career as a commander.

13 William Jacobs had been promoted to lieutenant in October 1813 and served aboard the *Bulwark* on the North American station in the last months of the War of 1812.

14 A pinnace is a light sailing vessel or a ship's boat.

15 The term "brigantine" refers to a two-masted vessel with her foremast entirely square-rigged and her mainmast rigged with a fore-and-aft mainsail—typically a gaff sail—and square topsails.

schooner laden with sugar, and then off again, after the Briganteen. We chased all that day and night, and next morning, we saw her rounding Nantucket shoals, and she escaped.

The morning after this, blowing pretty strong, and thick weather, we found a beautiful clipper schooner, close under our lee bow. She was too near us to escape, so she hove to. She was quite a new vessel, the *Thorn* from Baltimore, laden with flour. I was sent for to take her to Halifax, but I begged to be let off, as I had been so much away from the ship, and I thought I had a better chance of some work in the boats. So Uniacke[16] a passed Midshipman was sent instead of me, but I might just as well have gone, for a day or two after this, we recaptured a large English Brig, laden with Malaga wine and raisins, and I was packed off in her, and nine men, to take her to Halifax. I had a good passage, and rejoined my ship at Shelburne.

Soon after this, in September we joined a squadron under Admiral Edward Griffith[17] for an attack on Castine, on the Penobscot river. The squadron ran up in the night, Hyde Parker[18] in the *Tenedos* leading, and at daylight we came to an anchor off the Fort, which surrendered without firing a shot.

---

16 Uniacke, described by Aitchison as a passed midshipman, may well have been Lieutenant James Uniacke of the Royal Marines, who was killed at the Battle of Lake Borgne. It was not uncommon for an officer to hold a marine appointment at one rank and a navy appointment at another.

17 Edward Griffith entered the navy in 1778 and served aboard the *Royal George*. He saw continuous duty in Europe and the East Indies until 1812. Griffith became a rear admiral in August 1812 while commanding the North Sea Fleet and was soon sent to North America to assist Admiral John Borlase Warren. Soon after Griffith arrived in Halifax (November 1813), a hurricane blew in and damaged most of the British ships in port; he had only sixteen undamaged ships to maintain a blockade of the New England ports. In September 1814 Griffith and General Sir John Sherbrooke attacked and captured Castine, on the Massachusetts coast. (This territory became part of the new state of Maine in 1820.) From 1814 to 1817 and from 1819 to 1821 Warren commanded the British fleet at Halifax, Nova Scotia; he became a vice admiral in 1821 and retired soon thereafter, dying in 1832.

18 Hyde Parker, the eldest son of Sir Hyde Parker of Tredington in Worcestershire, became a lieutenant at age twenty in 1804, a commander two years later, and a captain in 1807. During the war with the United States, Parker commanded the 38-gun frigate *Tenedos*, which helped in the 1814 capture of Castine; in January 1815 his ship helped capture the American frigate *President*. Parker became a rear admiral in 1841, a vice admiral in 1852, and first sea lord of the Admiralty in 1853; he died in 1854.

American privateer escapes a British frigate during the War of 1812, engraving by Billings, from Capt. George Little, The American Cruiser *(Boston, 1846). Courtesy of the Naval Historical Center*

Remains of Fort Castine *from Benson J. Lossing,* The Pictorial Field-Book of the War of 1812 *(New York, 1869). British naval and land forces captured Castine in September 1814 before continuing up the Penobscot River in pursuit of the American sloop* Adams.

We learnt that the *Adams,*[19] an American Corvette,[20] had gone up to Bangor 20 miles higher, & a detachment was sent up to effect her destruction, or bring her away, the *Peruvian*[21] 18-gun brig commanding. I was in the *Bulwark*'s launch, a few troops were landed, which drove the Americans from their position, and as we approached the town, they set fire to the "*Adams,*" and she was destroyed by themselves. We returned to Castine after this service was over. *(1814 October)* It was a bloodless expedition and so much the better.[22]

We sent several prizes into Halifax from Castine, but they were of little value, and we went ourselves to Halifax, where we found the com-

19 The 28-gun frigate USS *Adams* was one of several ships constructed in 1799 at the onset of the Quasi-War with France. After serving during the first year of the Tripolitan War, the frigate was laid up out of commission at the Washington Navy Yard where she remained until the beginning of the war with Britain. During repairs the ship was razeed from a frigate to a sloop or corvette. Once the *Adams* escaped the British blockading fleet off the Virginia Capes in early 1814, she made several captures before retreating to the Penobscot River, where in September Captain Charles Morris destroyed her rather than allowing her to be captured by the British.

20 A corvette in the Age of Sail was a flush-decked warship with a single tier of guns, smaller than a frigate but ship-rigged on three masts. Corvettes were ideally suited for hot climates as the flush-deck construction permitted the free circulation of air.

21 HMS *Peruvian*, an 18-gun brig-sloop that carried 121 men, was launched in April 1808. She had an active career off the coast of North America during the War of 1812 before being broken up in February 1830.

22 The conquest of Bangor occurred with little American opposition; British forces remained there until April 27, 1815, well after the end of the war.

Sir Alexander Cochrane from Edward Pelham Brenton, The Naval History of Great
Britain *(London, 1837). Cochrane commanded the British North American station from
the spring of 1814 until the end of the war.*

mander in chief, Sir Alexander Cochrane[23] with his Flag in the *Tonnant*,[24]
and I received a letter from Lord Melville's secretary[25] to inform me that
I was recommended for promotion to Sir Alex Cochrane. Accordingly, I
was to quit the dear old *Bulwark* and all my shipmates, and last though
not least my friend the Captain who although he was very <u>gruff</u> at times,
I loved him dear. I joined the *Tonnant*, and it was sickening to see a Man-
of-War in such a state of lumber and confusion. We had about sixty in the
cockpit,[26] passed Midshipmen,[27] Assistant surgeons, clerks and some of
all sorts, a great many there like myself, on promotion, but few on the
Admiralty list, so that my chance for early promotion was good, but I
had still nearly 4 months to serve before I could undergo my examination.

It was now rumoured that the ships, which were collecting, were
destined to go with us first to the West Indies then to make an attack on

New Orleans. We were lumbered up with Artillery, horses, and every sort of warlike stores. We sailed a strong squadron, and steered straight to the West Indies. One night, a little Yankee schooner, confident in her own powers of sailing, came pretty nearly along side of us, and before we could get a gun ready to stop her (such was the abominable order we were in) she hauled off, and was soon out of gun shot. Next morning we saw her on our larboard beam, steering parallel to us, & just out of gun shot and she kept company the whole day, but we could not catch her.

[Aitchison sketched a boat, in pencil, before filling in this journal page.]

We touched at Guadeloupe and stayed a few days there, and then on to Jamaica, where we collected a convoy with troops, Black & White, and in coming out of Port Royal,[28] we very nearly left the *Tonnant* on

---

23 Alexander Forester Inglis Cochrane was the younger son of Thomas Cochrane, the eighth earl of Dundonald. He rose quickly through the naval ranks, making lieutenant in 1778 at age twenty, commander at age twenty-two, and captain in December 1782 at age twenty-four. In 1814 Vice Admiral Cochrane gained command of the British North American station, where he directed an aggressive campaign against the coast of the United States. Cochrane's aggressive tactics yielded mixed results: the conquest of Washington, D.C., but also unsuccessful forays against Baltimore and New Orleans. Cochrane encouraged American slaves to flee their masters and armed and trained those willing to take up arms against the United States; he also supported Native Americans in their war against the United States. After the war, Cochrane returned to England and remained in the service. He died in late January 1832.

24 HMS *Tonnant*, originally an 80-gun French ship-of-the-line, was captured in August 1798 at the Battle of the Nile. She joined the British North American squadron as Admiral Alexander Cochrane's flagship in the summer of 1814 and participated in the Chesapeake and New Orleans campaigns. The ship was broken up in March 1821.

25 Robert Saunders Dundas, second viscount Melville, was the first lord of the Admiralty; John W. Croker served as Melville's secretary.

26 The cockpit, or aft part of the orlop, was the space below the lower gundeck usually allotted as the living and eating space for midshipmen. During battle it served as the hospital area for wounded men because it was located beneath the waterline and was therefore less vulnerable to enemy fire.

27 A passed midshipman was one who had been rated but had not yet sat for his lieutenant's examination. See also chapter 1, note 14.

28 Port Royal, located in southeast Jamaica, was the fortified town and British naval base at the entrance to Kingston harbor.

the shoals, having run ashore in stays,[29] and with some difficulty we got her off again.

There was now no doubt of our going to make an attack on New Orleans, and I believe they were fully apprised of our approach and they were making every preparation for defense. In passing Negril Bay[30] (in Jamaica) we were joined by Sir Pulteney Malcolm,[31] in the *Royal Oak*,[32] with a number of troop ships and Transports with troops. We gathered size like a snowball as we approached the coast of Louisiana, and on getting off Pensacola, some Indian Chiefs came on board with Colonel Nicholls,[33] who was endeavoring to organize these Indians into some

---

29 When a sailing vessel is "in stays" it is in the act of going about or turning from one tack to another.

30 Negril Bay, a crescent-shaped cove bracketed by jutting spits of land eight miles apart, lies on the west end of the island of Jamaica.

31 Pulteney Malcolm from Burnfoot, Langholm, in Dumfriesshire joined the navy in 1778. Promoted to lieutenant in March 1783, he remained in the navy after the American War for Independence. Soon after war began with France in 1793, Malcolm won promotion to commander (April 1794) and to captain (October 1794). His ship, the *Donegal*, was damaged prior to the Battle of Trafalgar, but he arrived just in time to render assistance to the disabled British ships. Promoted to rear admiral in December 1813, Malcolm took command of the *Royal Oak* and transported a British army force from Bordeaux to North America; he acted as the third in command under Alexander Cochrane and George Cockburn. After the Battle of New Orleans, Malcolm returned to Europe and commanded a squadron in the North Sea in cooperation with the army under the Duke of Wellington. From 1816 to 1817 he commanded the St. Helena station which was responsible for enforcing a blockade of the island on which Napoleon had been exiled. Malcolm won promotion to vice admiral in 1821. He died in July 1838.

32 The 74-gun HMS *Royal Oak*, launched from Dudman, Deptford, in March 1809, saw considerable service in the Mediterranean. After the defeat of Napoleon in March 1814, the ship transported British troops from Bordeaux to North America, arriving in the late summer of 1814. The ship remained with Alexander Cochrane's squadron in the Chesapeake Bay and along the Gulf of Mexico until the British defeat at the Battle of New Orleans. The *Royal Oak* returned to the North Sea during the spring of 1815, supporting the British army in the defeat of Napoleon at Waterloo; it was broken up in Bermuda in 1850.

33 Edward Nicholls, a recently breveted colonel in the Royal Marines, had arrived in June 1814 on the Gulf Coast of the United States and established a British operational base at Prospect Bluff near the mouth of the Apalachicola River. He began arming and training Creek Indians and runaway slaves and in mid-September 1814 launched an unsuccessful attack against an American position at Mobile Point. Afterwards, Nicholls took his force to the Spanish Florida city of Pensacola where they remained until General Andrew Jackson captured the city in early November 1814.

sort of discipline. These Chiefs, or Kings as we called them, were received in great state by the Admiral. They were rigged out in gold-laced coats and cocked hats, but no shoes to their feet. After the formal reception and entertainment were over, the Midshipmen got them down below, and they got very drunk, and wound up by giving us the war whoop.

The expedition now swelled into a large squadron, and Troops, I don't know how many, under the command of Sir John Keane[34] (afterward Lord Keane) anchored off the Chandeleur Islands, a long distance from the Mouth of the Mississippi, prepared to disembark the Troops, a distance of 80 miles from the ships, but it was ascertained that there were Five American gunboats of great strength cruizing in the shoal waters, in our track to the point fixed upon for the disembarcation of the troops, so it was necessary either to capture or destroy them, before we ventured to expose troops in open boats, to the range of their guns.

Three divisions of boats under the command of Captain Lockyer[35] of the *Sophie*[36] started in pursuit of them. All our boats had passed mid-

---

34 John Keane was appointed a captain in the army in 1794 at age thirteen. In 1799 he joined an expedition to Gibraltar and Egypt; he served in Malta until 1803. Over the next decade Keane participated in British operations against Martinique and in the Pyrenees and Toulouse. Appointed major general in June 1814, he joined the operation against New Orleans in December 1814. On December 25, 1814, Generals Sir Edward Pakenham and Samuel Gibbs—both of whom died during the British attack at Chalmette on January 8, 1815—superseded him. Keane participated in the British capture of Fort Bowyer in February 1815 before joining the Duke of Wellington in Paris that summer. He later served as commander in chief at Bombay. Keane died in August 1844.

35 Nicholas Lockyer had served in the Mediterranean, in the English Channel, and at Newfoundland before being promoted to lieutenant in December 1803. He won promotion to commander because of his bravery off the coast of Santo Domingo in September 1806. Lockyer gained command of the *Sophie* and served in the Chesapeake and along the Gulf Coast during the War of 1812. Chosen to lead the British assault against the American gunboats on Lake Borgne, he was seriously wounded; the successful attack won for Lockyer a promotion to captain, a rank he held until his death in February 1847.

36 HMS *Sophie*, an 18-gun brig-sloop launched from Pelham, Frindsbury, in September 1809, was active in British operations along the Gulf of Mexico in 1814 and supported British operations against New Orleans. She was sold in August 1825 in the East Indies.

shipmen in them, as well as Lieutenants, so I was excluded, as I had not passed. They soon got sight of the gunboats, which were at anchor, close to a small island, and moored head to stern. Our boats pulled up with a strong tide against them, but the *Commodore*[37] was boarded by Lockyer in his gig, who was cut down, as well as almost every man in his boat. They were however soon overpowered, and all fell one after the other as the boats came up. My poor shipmate, Rob Uniacke,[38] lost a leg, and died after the amputation, and another, O'Reilly,[39] lost his eye. He is still a Lieutenant. These gunboats were all commissioned and Lieutenants appointed to command them. They were found useful in navigating these shoal waters of the Bay of Catalan,[40] I believe they called it. We now began to assemble the troops about half way between the final landing place, and the ships, on a small low swampy island, Pearl Island, covered with a sort of Bull rush.

I was very unhappy at my chance of not getting up with the troops, but I succeeded at last by hook or by crook, by being sent in charge of the Captain of the Fleet's gig, Sir Edward Codrington's[41] with his valet

---

37 The *Commodore* was Lieutenant Thomas ap Catesby Jones's gunboat.

38 In this instance Aitchison refers to Uniacke as Rob. James Uniacke lost a leg at the Battle of Lake Borgne and subsequently died. Rob may have been his middle name or perhaps a nickname.

39 John O'Reilly, a midshipman during the Battle of Lake Borgne, was promoted to lieutenant in November 1815; he remained at that rank for the remainder of his career, as Aitchison remarks.

40 Aitchison refers to the southwestern arm of Lake Borgne, into which flowed Bayou Catalan, or Catiline—known today as Bayou Bienvenue. The bayou was then a small creek that extended from Lake Borgne through the middle of a reed morass towards the Mississippi River, some ten miles south of New Orleans.

41 Edward Codrington, from Dodington in Gloucestershire, entered the navy in 1783. He became a lieutenant in May 1793 after having served on the Halifax, Mediterranean, and home stations. Promoted to commander in October 1794 and to captain in April 1795, Codrington participated in the Battle of Trafalgar. He joined the North American station in early 1814 and gained promotion to rear admiral in early June. Codrington acted as Cochrane's captain of the fleet during the Chesapeake campaign (summer 1814) and the campaign against New Orleans (December 1814-January 1815). He became a vice admiral in 1825 and Admiral of the Blue in 1837; he remained in active service until December 31, 1842. Codrington died in late April 1851.

& shoe brushes, I believe, but I did not mind that, for it made my chance better of staying with the Army. Well I went to Pearl Island also, and although we had roughish work of it, sleeping in the open boats, with only our sails for a covering, and salt provisions, which hunger sometimes compelled us to eat two days' dinner at once. We had a very merry time of it, and Sir James Gordon,[42] the Captain of the *Seahorse*,[43] who had lost a leg a few years before, was full of fun, and had generally a group of Midshipmen round him listening and laughing at his jokes.

When preparations were completed, we started for the Mouth of the Creek,[44] which we were to enter and which creek ended about 8 miles below New Orleans, and was navigable for boats to within 3 miles of the Mississippi. It was about 9 miles from the mouth of it to this point. It was very tortuous and the banks on each side covered with these long reeds, indicating the swampy nature of the ground, which was quite flat. There was a Fisherman's hut near the mouth of the creek, and our boats which went to reconnoiter, found it occupied by an American picquet,[45] which retreated when the boats came near. The advance Guard of the

---

42 James Gordon of Wardhouse joined the navy in 1793. After service on a variety of ships on many different stations, he won promotion to lieutenant in January 1800. Promoted to commander in 1803 and to captain in 1805, Gordon served primarily in the Mediterranean and Adriatic. In March 1811, while participating in an engagement off the coast of Lissa, he was severely wounded, having had a leg shot off at the knee. Gordon spent the next two years recovering before joining Alexander Cochrane off the coast of North America in the spring of 1814. During the fall campaign against the United States, Gordon commanded a squadron that captured Alexandria, Virginia. He later played a minor role in the operations against New Orleans. Gordon served on the North American and the Mediterranean stations before winning promotion to rear admiral in January 1837, to vice admiral in January 1854, and to Admiral of the Fleet in January 1868. He spent his career from 1840 to 1853 as the lieutenant governor of Greenwich Hospital, after which he became the institution's governor. He remained at that post until his death in January 1869.

43 HMS *Seahorse*, a 38-gun frigate commissioned in June 1794, served as a support vessel during the British operations against New Orleans. The ship remained on duty until she was broken up in July 1819.

44 The creek to which Aitchison refers was the Villeré Canal, which stretched some three miles through prairies and woods to the Mississippi River, ten miles south of New Orleans.

45 The term picquet or picket refers to a soldier or group of soldiers serving as a forward lookout against an enemy advance.

James Alexander Gordon, engraving from the Naval Chronicle *(London, 1814). Courtesy of the Naval Historical Center. Captain Gordon served on the British North American station under Vice Admiral Alexander Cochrane. Aitchison found Gordon to be "full of fun" when their paths crossed at New Orleans.*

Army went right up to the head of the Creek, and took up a position among some sugar plantations, 8 miles below the city, but I have no business to attempt to describe what the army did, and I possibly would make many mistakes. All that I wish is, to acquaint my children, what part I acted in these juvenile days.

We kept a fire burning at the Mouth of the Creek, during the night, and one night it fell to my lot to go down with my boat's crew, and keep it up, and I took very good care to keep a glorious blaze of light, not only for the sake of our boats, coming up with soldiers, but because we were not

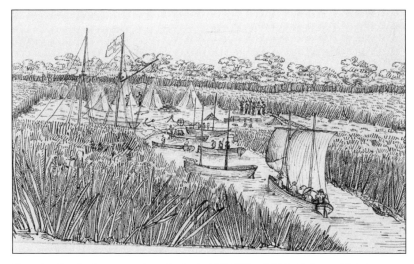

Boats landing in the swamps from Logbook of HMS Royal Oak, *Pulteney Malcolm Papers, William L. Clements Library, University of Michigan. Rear Admiral Pulteney Malcolm's ink drawing depicts British forces at the mouth of Lake Borgne. The British proceeded from this site, known as the Fisherman's Village, through swamps and low lying prairies to a point nine miles south of New Orleans, where they established camp on the banks of the Mississippi River.*

a little afraid that some stray alligator, or some other brute inhabiting these swamps, might make a meal of us before we were aware of it. I was glad when daylight came, and that duty ceased. I was now transferred to a larger boat, and assisted in landing troops & hauling up guns to the front, and any other odd job that poor Jack[46] was put to when serving ashore. The weather the whole of the six weeks I slept in the open boat was bitterly cold, and many of the Blacks who came from the West Indies with us died of cold. That winter December 1814 was unusually severe, but we found oranges still on the trees, and as the storehouses, which our

---

46 Jack or Jack-tar was a slang expression for a British naval seaman. Tar is short for tarpaulin, the tarred canvas that seamen used to protect themselves from foul weather. Originally the name was applied only to men whose station on the ship was on the masts and yards.

troops occupied, were full of sugar, we converted these oranges, into good wholesome Marmalade, and this stuff helped to "fill up the chinks." Constant skirmishes were going on, between our troops and the Americans, but we had got a firm footing, and they were invariably beaten back.

The Americans had taken up a strong position. On one flank was the noble River Mississippi, and on the other the low morass, and from the one to the other they had thrown up an embankment formed of mud, great baulks of wood, and bags of cotton with a broad ditch, with water in it, all along. We threw up some redoubts to molest them, with breastworks made of sugar, thinking, I imagine, that the sugar would be equally as effective as sand, but they soon showed us the contrary. They knocked the batteries about our ears, and poor Jack was ordered up to bring away the guns. This was the dirtiest, and the most fatigueing job I ever was engaged in. I had been in the boat bringing up troops all the night, before, and we were just making ourselves comfortable for the night—i.e. we had a tub in the boat, which was half filled with earth, and on this we kindled a fire, which pretty well smoke dried us, after the boat's sail was over us. We were already fatigued, but we were obliged to go. The roads were muddy, and I remember to this day how wretchedly off I was about the shoes, which stuck in the mud every now & then, and I was so tired, I felt half inclined to leave my heavy great coat in the mud, but we stuck together and went on. The night was pitch dark, and when we reached these guns, which we were to drag out of the mud, we found it an impossibility. The commander of the army, Sir Edward Pakenham,[47] came to us, tried all he could, sometimes with threats, other times warning, but it would not do, and finally a large working party, fresh & strong, had to do that which our party had not strength to do *(1814 Decr.)*. I believe I slept in the mud the remainder of the night, and daylight found me in a horrid mess. I was rejoiced as were my crew, to get back to our own home, by our mud tub and our canvass covering, and clean ourselves as best we could.

Preparations were now making for the grand attack on the Enemy's lines. We had been waiting for reinforcements which had arrived, accompanied by three distinguished Peninsular generals [Here Aitchison inserts a sketch of the British and American lines.] viz. Sir Edward Pakenham,

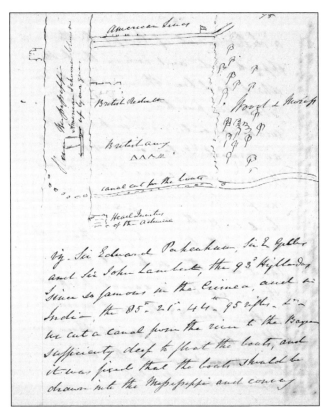

Sketch of British and American lines with canal cut indicated. Aitchison makes note of the "American Schooner blown up by our guns" on the Mississippi River; British forces destroyed the USS Carolina *on the morning of December 27, 1814.*

47 Edward Michael Pakenham, born at Longford Castle in Westmeath County, became a lieutenant in May 1794 at the age of sixteen and was promoted to captain a few days later. He participated in the Irish rebellion in 1798, winning promotion to major. In October 1799 Pakenham became a lieutenant colonel and participated in the British reduction of the Danish and Swedish West India Islands. He had risen quickly through the ranks, but his rise accelerated after his sister married the Duke of Wellington in 1806; Pakenham joined Wellington in the peninsular campaign, winning fame and a promotion for his actions at the Battle of Salamanca in July 1812. He arrived in North America in December 1814, just in time to command the land operations at the Battle of New Orleans; Pakenham died on January 8, 1815, in the British attack against Jackson's line at Chalmette.

Sir Samuel Gibbs,[48] and Sir John Lambert,[49] the 93d Highlanders, since so famous in the Crimea, and in India, the 85th, 21st, 44th, 95th rifles [illegible]. We cut a canal from the river to the Bayou sufficiently deep to float the boats, and it was fixed that the boats should be drawn into the Mississippi and convey a detachment of troops to the opposite side, and carry the batteries which had been thrown up to enfilade our position. While these arrangements were in progress, an armed schooner[50] dropped down river, and opened fire on our camp, which was almost on a level with the river (indeed the river is oftentimes higher than the land on either side, but banks thrown up like a canal keep it within bounds). The next morning, the artillery brought up their guns and silenced this schooner, which soon after blew up.

---

48 Samuel Gibbs joined the army in 1783 and over the next two decades served in North America, England, the Mediterranean, Gibraltar, and the Caribbean. In 1810 he became a colonel and soon participated in British operations against Java and India. Promoted to major general in June 1813, Gibbs served as General Sir Edward Pakenham's second in command during the 1814-15 New Orleans campaign. During the January 8, 1815, attack Gibbs commanded one of the main columns involved in the frontal assault. He suffered severe wounds and died the following day.

49 John Lambert joined the army as an ensign in July 1791 and served at Valenciennes, Lincelles, and Dunkirk in October 1793; he helped suppress the Irish Rebellion of 1798, and participated in the New Holland expedition of 1799-1800, in the Portuguese and Spanish operations of 1808-9, and in operations in the Netherlands in 1809. Lambert joined Wellington's army in 1811, won promotion to major general in June 1813, and fought at Nivelles, Nive, Orthes, and Toulouse. After Robert Ross's death at Baltimore, Lambert joined the British force at New Orleans where he commanded Pakenham's reserves. Lambert succeeded to command after Pakenham's death, called off the attack at New Orleans, and commanded the last land operation of the war— the capture of Fort Bowyer. He returned to Europe in time to participate with Wellington's army at Waterloo; Lambert died in September 1847.

50 Commander Daniel Todd Patterson had used the 14-gun schooner *Carolina* to maintain control of the Mississippi River and to harass British forces encamped on the river's bank. Yet the river's heavy current combined with a lack of wind prevented Patterson from evacuating the ship upriver before British troops brought in heavy artillery. On the morning of December 27, 1814, British artillery fired hot shot (cannon balls heated red hot) that lodged in the *Carolina*'s wooden walls, setting fires that quickly ignited a store of powder. Patterson evacuated his crew before the ship exploded—only one American was killed and six were wounded.

[Margin note:] The banks to keep the Mississippi within bounds are called Levées and are often 8 feet high, the river having raised its bed a considerable height above the level of the surrounding country, and New Orleans is drained into Lake Pontchartrain.

(1815)

THE 8 JANUARY was the day fixed upon for the assault on the enemy's lines. At daylight the boats were dragged into the canal ready to convey the 85th Reg[iment] and other detachments of troops to the other side of the Mississippi, which were intended to carry the batteries on that side which enfiladed our troops. My boat embarked part of the flank company of the 85th and pulled to the other side, where we landed them and returned for more.

A Rocket at Daylight was the signal for the assault, which took place immediately, but our troops encountered such a murderous fire at the edge of the ditch that they fell back without crossing it and in 15 minutes about 1800 men were put 'hors de combat' [out of combat]. The Commander in Chief Pakenham killed, General Gibbs killed & Keane wounded. On our side of the river the Batteries were carried, but in the course of the day we abandoned them and all returned and occupied the same ground we held in the morning. It was a disastrous affair from beginning to end and it was melancholy indeed to listen to the details of all the misfortunes, which had happened to many of those who we had seen in health and strength a few hours before. The 93d Highlanders, a fine veteran Regiment but recently arrived from the Cape stood up as they always did without flinching, and marched to the ditch, as I have heard, in the highest order, but they were compelled to retreat with 600 killed & wounded. Our Naval part of the force suffered but a trifling loss among the small armed men.

It was determined to give up any further attempt upon New Orleans.

I was sent down to the *Tonnant* and had just time given me to collect my ideas before I was ordered one morning and very unexpectedly

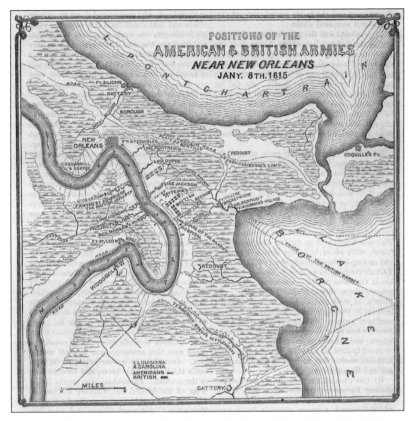

Positions of the American & British Armies Near New Orleans Jany. 8th. 1815,
1864. The Historic New Orleans Collection (1974.25.5.68)

on board the *Plantagenet*[51] to undergo my examination. I was put into a
tremendous castle.[52] They were cleaning the cockpit where all the chests
were in confusion and amidst all the dirt & dust I was obliged to seek
out mine to clean myself and dress myself for this serious affair. However
after sundry messages coming down to me "to bear a hand the boat was
waiting alongside" I got away [with] logs, certificates and all in a high state

of perspiration, my face, I imagine, covered with sand, but I had no glass to look at it on board. I went and found my "Passing Captains" were to be Tristram Robert Ricketts,[53] Pearce[54] & Lloyd.[55] They had not assembled, so I was asked below to the Midshipmen's berth, and just as I began to swallow some pea soup the Quarter Master came down & bellowed out that "I was wanted in the Cabin." I knew what that meant, so I collected my documents & appeared before these Big Wigs who commenced by examining my logs, certificates &c. and then various questions were put to me in Navigation and Seamanship, all of which I had the good fortune to answer satisfactorily and finally I received my Passing Certificate and was complimented by the Captains, two of whom said they would feel happy to have me for a Lieutenant. And Ricketts did apply to the Admiral for me and [the] next day I was appointed acting Lieutenant of the *Vengeur*[56] 74, Captain Ricketts. I had no uniform, nothing but my chest & that scantily furnished but I took leave of my messmates and entered at once in my new career, very happy indeed. I found there an acting Lieutenant like my Andrew Forbes, a gentlemanly good fellow whose friendship I enjoyed for many years.

---

51 HMS *Plantagenet*, a 74-gun ship-of-the-line launched from Woolwich in August 1801, served as a support and transport ship during the New Orleans campaign; she was broken up in May 1817, shortly after the end of the war.

52 The term castle refers to the space between the short-raised forecastle deck and the main deck at the bow. It was the traditional living space for ordinary sailors.

53 Tristram Robert Ricketts had been promoted to captain in November 1801 and would ultimately reach the rank of vice admiral before his death in August 1842.

54 Joseph Pearce served along the Chesapeake during the early part of the War of 1812. In the summer of 1814 he was promoted to captain and sent with Admiral Alexander Cochrane to the Gulf Coast.

55 Robert Lloyd had been a Royal Navy captain since December 1799. In the fall of 1814 he was sent to the Gulf Coast to assist with the British invasion of Louisiana; in January 1837 Lloyd reached the rank of vice admiral.

56 HMS *Vengeur* was a 74-gun ship-of-the-line launched from Graham, Harwich, in June 1810. Like the *Plantagenet*, the *Vengeur* served as a support and transport ship at New Orleans; Captain Ricketts served as her commander during this campaign. The *Vengeur* became a receiving ship in February 1824 and remained as such until she was broken up in August 1843.

The *Vengeur* was almost immediately ordered with a Squadron & troops down to the Pensacola coast to take Fort Boyer[57] at the entrance of Mobile river. I landed in command of the *Vengeur*'s small arms men, and we pitched our huts among the low sand hills about this Fort. Our duty was principally to act as a working party in carrying up shot &c. to our advanced Batteries. This sort of work rather disgusted us but it did not last long. After our guns were ready to open, the Fort surrendered and the garrison marched out and lay their arms down with all the honors of war.

We were now sent to Dauphin Island, which was quite a paradise in comparison with the sand hills and here we made huts for ourselves with boughs of spruce, which were quite fragrant. It was here that we heard that a treaty of Peace[58] had been signed between Eng[land] and the United States and we were all ordered on board. I got for my duties with the "small arms men" £42 as forage money, which was very acceptable, especially as I found when I got on board that my trunks had been robbed of 70 dollars and as my servant boy had the key, I had every reason to believe that he was the thief. My cot & cabin was occupied by one of the American officers who was taken at the Fort and I was very glad when an order came to send them all way released. We now, Feb. 1815, sailed for old England, touching at the Havanah where we stayed a

---

57 Fort Bowyer—located at Mobile Point, commanding the entrance to Mobile Bay—was constructed in the spring of 1813 after General James Wilkinson had taken the city from the Spanish. The fort served as Mobile's chief defense until July 1814 when it was evacuated. A month later Andrew Jackson ordered Fort Bowyer reoccupied and reinforced; on September 12 the fort withstood a combined British army-navy attack in which the flagship of the naval assault, the 22-gun sloop *Hermes*, ran aground in the shallow water of Mobile Bay and had to be destroyed. British forces returned to Mobile Bay in early February 1815, after the debacle at New Orleans, and forced the surrender of Fort Bowyer on February 11.

58 Although American and British diplomats had signed the Treaty of Ghent in Belgium on December 24, 1814, the war did not officially end until both governments ratified the agreement on February 17, 1815. Four days before ratification—and two days after the surrender of Fort Bowyer—news of the treaty reached the Gulf Coast, sparing Mobile from further attack.

few days, giving us an opportunity of going out into the country and saw the manufacture of cigars going on at Woodvilles.[59] I thought it a very nice town and a splendid harbour.

We next touched at Bermuda and took in water and then sailed for Plymouth, arriving there after a fine run of 16 days. We fully expected to be paid off immediately but to our surprise in getting into Causand Bay[60] we heard that Bonaparte was in France again, and having escaped from Elba, he was at the head of a large Army, almost all having given in their adhesion to him. I was confirmed to my lieutenancy on the 6th May, & to the *Vengeur* we sailed on a cruize off Ushant[61] and when [in] June we arrived all was excitement as the French Army was advancing into Belgium. In the course of time, accounts of the battle of Waterloo came and a general order was issued to every cruizer strictly to examine all outward bound ships lest Boney [Bonaparte] might be found on board making his escape. We had a chain of Men-of-War extending from Cape Finisterre across the Bay of Biscay to the Scilly Islands[62] within signal distance of each other. I was then Junior Lieutenant & Signal Lieutenant and my duty was to be up all day which at this time, the end of June, was from about 2:30 am till about 9 pm. So I was pretty well done up by the time the day was over as I had to report every vessel, & we examined an immense number of them. We stood over to the Scilly Islands to get beef & vegetables, and here we heard that the Great Napoleon was actu-

---

59 Woodvilles probably refers to a cigar-producing facility owned by Londoner William Woodville. Although the Spanish government did not permit the export of tobacco from Cuba, except to Spain, foreigners were permitted to set up trading shops and production facilities, and Woodville's shop became one of the most important.

60 Causand (usually Cawsand) Bay is located on the southwestern side of Plymouth Sound. Sheltered by Rame Head Peninsula to the southwest, it is protected from heavy violent southwestern gales, making it an ideal anchorage for ships waiting to enter Plymouth.

61 Ushant is a small island off the coast of Brittany in northwest France.

62 The Scilly Islands lie to the south and west of Penzance off the southwest coast of England.

ally on board the *Bellerophon*.[63] He had given himself up to Captain Maitland,[64] and was then in Plymouth Sound. So on our anchoring in the Sound there we found him, and shoals of boats lying off, trying to get a glimpse of the great man. I cannot say I ever saw him. We were close to him, but of course we could not well make him out, & he did not much like to show himself.

---

63 HMS *Bellerophon*, a 74-gun, line-of-battle ship commissioned in October 1786, served off the coast of France during the Napoleonic Wars. She gained fame as the ship that accepted Napoleon aboard as a prisoner. The *Bellerophon* was converted to a prison ship in October 1815. She was renamed *Captivity* in October 1824 and was sold in January 1836.

64 Frederick Lewis Maitland, born at Rankeilour in Fife, became a lieutenant in 1795, shortly before his eighteenth birthday. After serving in the North Sea, in the Mediterranean, and at Gibraltar, Maitland gained promotion to commander in June 1799; he became a captain in March 1801. During the war with the United States, Maitland commanded on the Halifax and West India stations; he was collecting ships for a voyage to North America when the war ended in 1815. Learning in May of that year that Napoleon had returned to France, Maitland positioned himself off the coast of Rochefort and soon found that Napoleon wanted passage to the United States. Maitland refused to grant passage, agreeing instead to transport Napoleon to England. On July 15, 1815, Napoleon boarded the *Bellerophon* as a prisoner of the British government. Maitland later commanded in the South Atlantic, in the Mediterranean, and in the East Indies. He became a rear admiral in July 1830 and died at sea in November 1839.

Color Plates

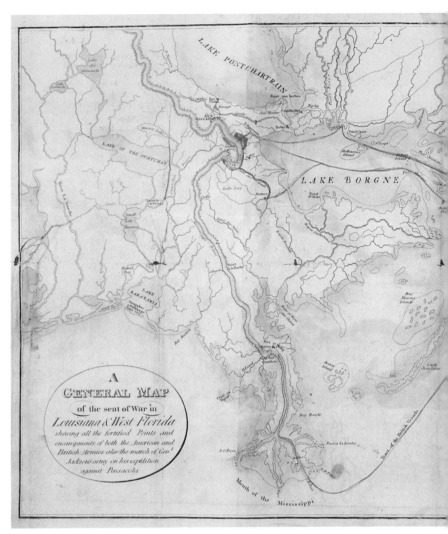

A General Map of the seat of War in Louisiana & West Florida . . . *by Arsène LaCarrière Latour, 1815. The Historic New Orleans Collection (1980.32)*

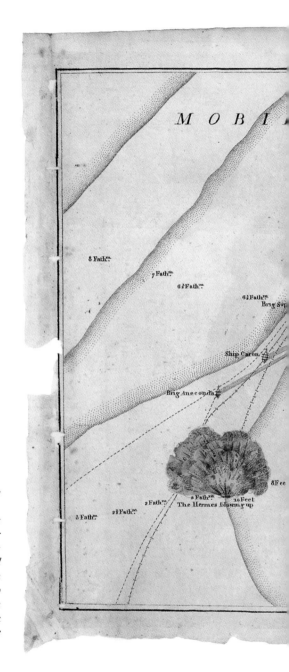

British attack on Fort Bowyer by Arsène LaCarrière Latour, 1815. The Historic New Orleans Collection (1979.238.1). Latour misidentifies the date of the attack; the battle depicted here occurred in 1814, not 1815, as a lead-in to the campaign against New Orleans. During the operation American cannon fire sank HMS Hermes, *forcing the British to break off the attack.*

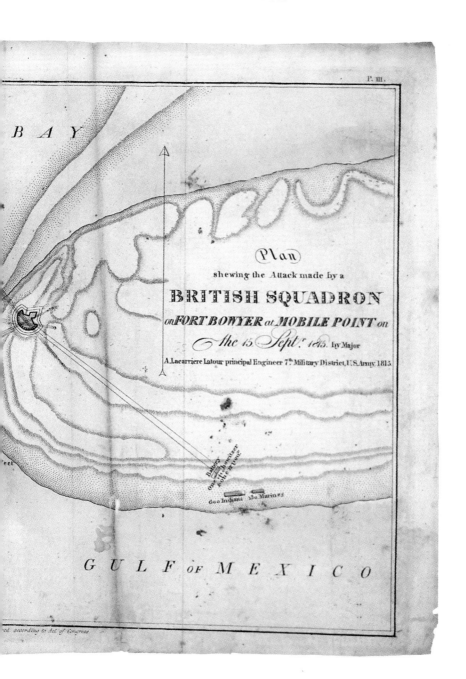

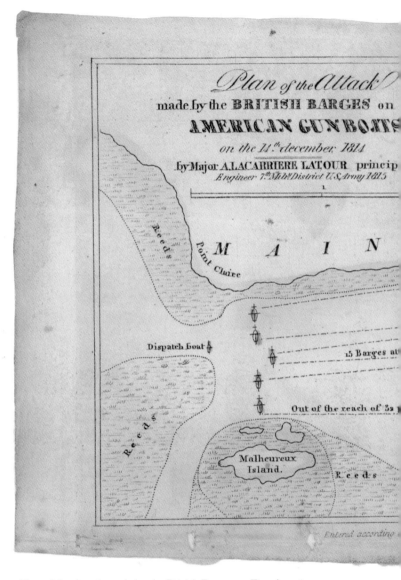

Plan of the Attack made by the British Barges on Five American
Gunboats on the 14th december, 1814 *by Arsène LaCarrière Latour, 1815.*
The Historic New Orleans Collection (1979.238.2)

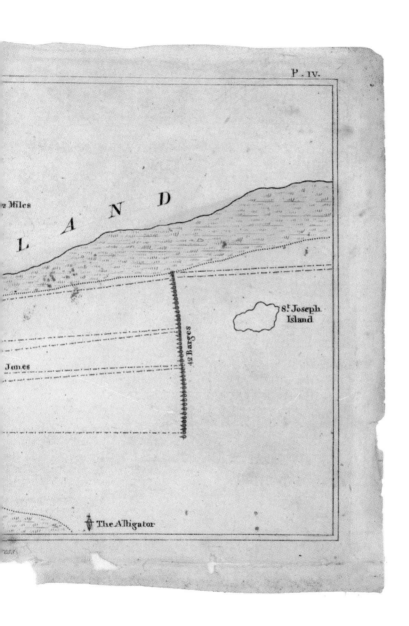

Battle of Lake Borgne by Thomas L. Hornbrook. The Historic New Orleans Collection (1950.54)

Capture of American Gun Vessels off New Orleans Decr. 1814 *by Lieutenant William Hole, December 1814. The Historic New Orleans Collection (1969.4). Depicting the Battle of Lake Borgne, this watercolor shows five American gunboats commanded by Lieutenant Thomas ap Catesby Jones surrounded by thirty-three British brigs and sloops commanded by Captain Nicholas Lockyer.*

Map Shewing the Landing of the British Army its several Encampments and Fortifications on the Mississippi and the Works they erected on their Retreat . . . *by Arsène LaCarrière Latour, 1815. The Historic New Orleans Collection (1979.238.7). The navigation of Lake Borgne, Bayou Bienvenu, and Villeré Canal permitted the British to reach the Mississippi River without opposition, greatly surprising General Andrew Jackson.*

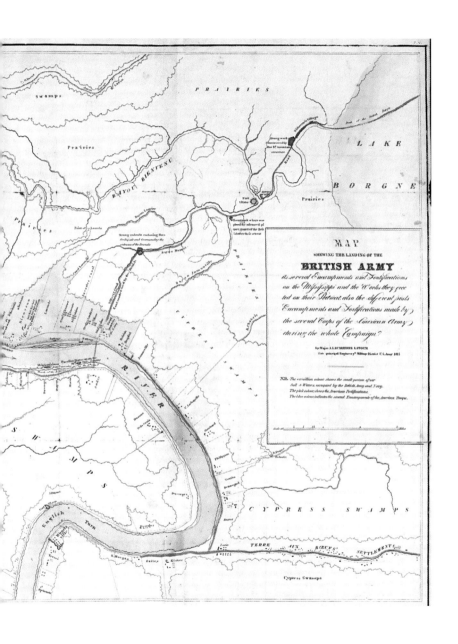

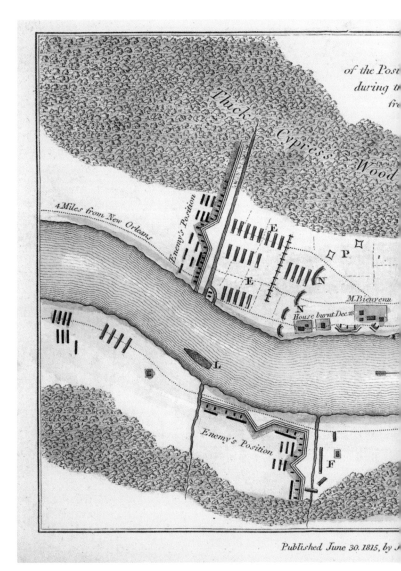

Sketch of the Position of the British and American Forces, during the
Operations against New Orleans, from 23ᵈ Decʳ 1814, to 18ᵗʰ Janʸ 1815.
The Historic New Orleans Collection (1971.98), bequest of Richard Koch

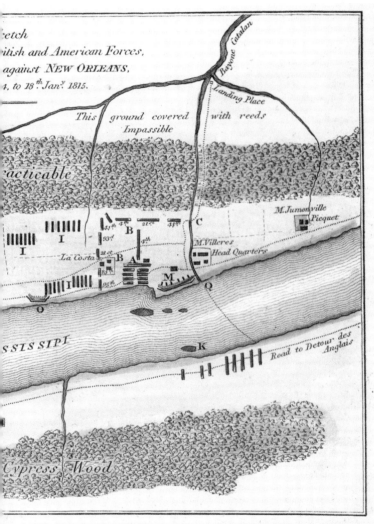

A PRIVATE of the 5ᵗʰ WEST INDIA REGIMENT.

A Private of the 5th West India Regiment. *National Army Museum, Chelsea.*
Aitchison observed that many Black troops—such as those from the 5th West India
Regiment—suffered greatly from the cold and damp during the New Orleans campaign.

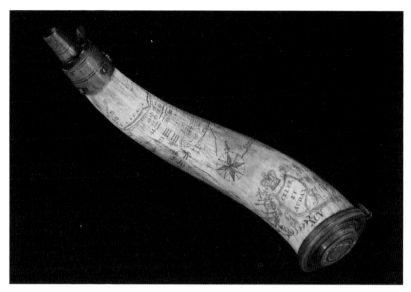

Scrimshaw powder horn issued by the British army depicting the Battle of New Orleans. The William C. Cook War of 1812 in the South Collection, The Historic New Orleans Collection (2002-36-L). The horn's owner, a member of the elite 95th Rifle Regiment, carefully inscribed a map of the battlefield and the regimental motto Celer et Audux *(Swift and Bold).*

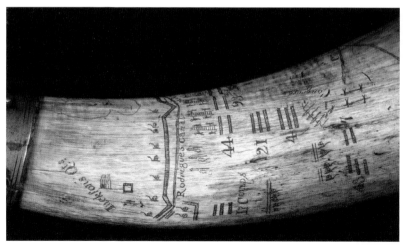

Detail of powder horn

Death of Pakenham at the Battle of New Orleans, *Felix Octavius Carr Darley (delineator), W. Ridgway (engraver), between 1854 and 1860. The Historic New Orleans Collection (1958.37), gift of Boyd Cruise. In this romanticized view the 93rd Highlanders, incorrectly depicted in oddly colored kilts, support the dying general. Aitchison's description of the battle includes reference to the valiant efforts of this military regiment: "The 93d Highlanders, a fine veteran Regiment . . . stood up as they always did without flinching, and marched to the ditch, as I have heard, in the highest order, but they were compelled to retreat with 600 killed & wounded."*

Fort Bowyer flying a British flag from Logbook of HMS Royal Oak, *Pulteney Malcolm Papers, William L. Clements Library, University of Michigan. The American fort, which protected the entrance to Mobile Bay, formally capitulated to the British on February 12, 1815; the next day news of the Treaty of Ghent reached the Gulf Coast, sparing Mobile from further attack.*

Scene in Plymouth Sound in August 1815: The "Bellerophon" with Napoleon
Aboard at Plymouth (26 July-4 August 1815) *by John James Chalon, 1816-17.*
© *National Maritime Museum, London. Napoleon surrendered to Captain
Frederick Maitland of HMS* Bellerophon *on July 15, 1815. On July 26 the
ship sailed into Plymouth Sound with Napoleon aboard as a prisoner. Aitchison
commented on the "shoals of boats lying off, trying to get a glimpse of the great man."*

The Bombardment of
Algiers, 27 August 1816
*by George Chambers, Sr.,
1836. © National
Maritime Museum,
London. Lord Viscount
Exmouth's August 1816
attack on Algiers dealt a
crippling blow to the power
of the Barbary pirates.
Aitchison served on HMS*
Leander *during the
Algerian campaign.*

A View of Louisburg in North America, taken from the Light House
when that City was beseiged [*sic*] in 1758. © *National Maritime Museum,
London. Louisbourg (the original French spelling is now standard) had been
one of the most important French fortifications in North America prior to the
British capture during the French and Indian War. By the time Aitchison
visited in 1817, the fort had been dismantled and only a few huts remained.*

the **Light Houfe** *when that City was befeiged in 1758.*
N.º 69 in S.ᵗ Pauls Church Yard, London.

The Square, St George's, Bermuda, *Emily Phillips, artist and engraver, Capt. Hackett, engraver.* © *National Maritime Museum, London. The picturesque city of St. George's, with its white buildings and evergreen trees, served as Bermuda's capital until 1816. Aitchison spent the winter of 1817-18 in Bermuda with Admiral Sir David Milne.*

Capt.ᵗ Hackell, Lith. Exeter

, Sᵀ George's, Bermuda.

Jumping Jenny Landing Her Cargo. © *National Maritime Museum, London. Smuggling remained a constant problem along isolated stretches of the English coastline after the Napoleonic Wars. As captain of the* Clio *from 1826 to 1827— the only command post he ever held—Aitchison tracked smugglers in the North Sea.*

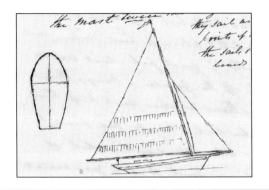

CHAPTER 3

A Seasoned Officer, 1815–1827

.

(1815)

In August we went round to Portsmouth, and in to the harbour and were paid off, and in September I went home, and remained on half pay all the winter, and attended to the lectures at the College in Edin[burgh], on Chemistry, Natural Philosophy, & Natural History. *(1816)* Early in the spring, Admiral Milne was appointed to the command on the North American Station, and I was appointed to his Flag ship *Leander*,[1] 60, Captain Chetham. We joined her at Sheerness. My old friend & shipmate Dewar, one of the Midshipmen Dick Baird another & many others of the active young friends, on our arrival at Portsmouth, we got all ready to start for our station, but all of a sudden, our determination was suddenly changed.

Lord Exmouth[2] was ordered to Algiers, to chastise the Algerines and we were ordered to put ourselves under his orders, Admiral Milne to go second in command. The account of this expedition is well detailed in the history of the country, the part we took in the *Leander*, was a very distinguished one. Running in, close to Lord Exmouth's Ship,[3] we

---

1 HMS *Leander*, a 58-gun frigate launched in November 1813, was the second ship of that name to serve in the British navy. The original 52-gun *Leander* was captured by the French in August 1798 and recaptured by the Russians at Corfu in March 1799. Returned to the Royal Navy, the original *Leander* served on the North American station and in April 1806 was responsible for firing on an American merchant ship in New York harbor, an episode that almost brought the United States and Britain to war. In early 1813 the original *Leander* was renamed *Hygeia*. The second *Leander*, commanded by Captain Edward Chetham, participated in the August 27, 1816, attack on Algiers; the frigate lost 17 men, and 118 were wounded.

2 Having reached the rank of Admiral of the Blue and risen to the peerage as Baron Exmouth in 1814, Edward Pellew added further laurels to his name when he successfully led the British squadron against Algiers, winning the release of all Christian slaves there. Pellew remained in the navy, becoming Vice Admiral of the United Kingdom in February 1832; he died the following January. See also chapter 1, note 70.

3 Lord Exmouth's ship, HMS *Queen Charlotte*, a 104-gun ship-of-the-line, was launched from Deptford in May 1810. During the Battle of Algiers, the ship, commanded by Captain James Brisbane, served as the operation's flagship, mooring within eighty yards of the mole-head battery that guarded the entrance to the harbor. At this range the weight of the ship's guns quickly overwhelmed the shore batteries of the pirates, permitting the British fleet to enter the harbor and destroy the Algerian fleet.

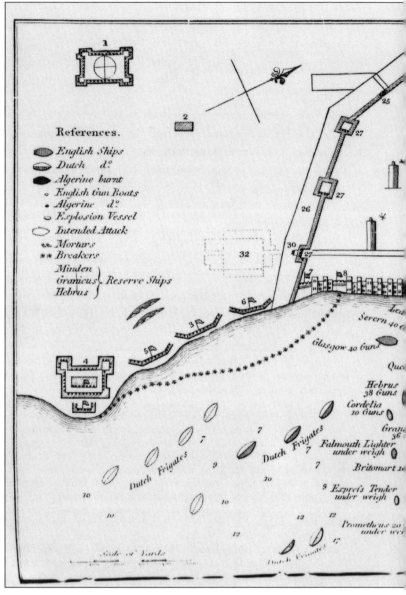

Map of Lord Viscount Exmouth's August 1816 attack against Algiers from the Naval Chronicle (London, 1817). Courtesy of the Naval Historical Center

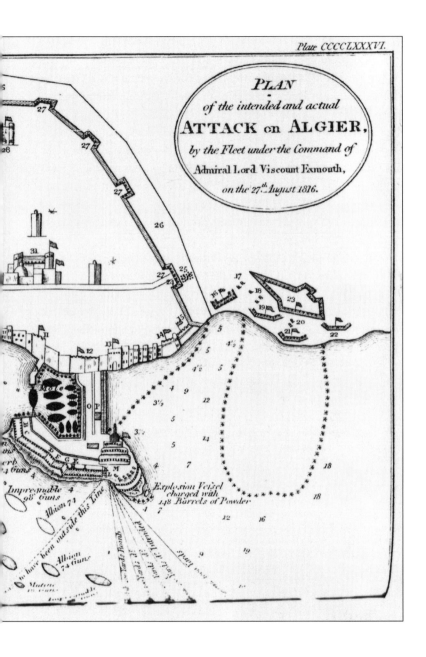

anchored at the mouth of the mole,[4] within 90 yards of the shore, and under the guns of the Fah machet,[5] with 50 row boats ready to board us.

Admiral Milne had shifted his Flag for the occasion [into] the *Impregnable*,[6] Captain Brace,[7] and she was terribly mauled, having had 210 men killed & wounded.

The guns I had charge of were on the upper deck, 42-pound carronades on the gangway, & Forecastle, and on commencing Action, our attention was directed to these row boats, and we poured into them, such a destructive fire of grape shot with one broadside, they were literally annihilated. The action continued 9 hours, the *Leander* was under a fire of musketry the whole time. I have often thought how mercifully I was preserved through this long period on the upper deck, in uniform, epaulette on, the men for 20 minutes lying down at their quarters, no smoke about the ship, walking by myself, on the gangway, a fair target to the fellows behind the walls. I was never hit. The Captain & First Lieutenant on the 2nd deck, walking about too, were equally preserved. We had ceased firing for this period for the boats had gone into the Mole, in our line of fire, to set fire to the Algerine Squadron, which they did in gallant style, suffering severely. I had one gun cleared at my quarters, every man either killed or wounded, 2 midshipmen killed and 2 wounded.

---

4 A mole is a long pier or breakwater forming part of the sea defenses of a port; it can be free standing or have one end connected to the shore. In the case of Algiers, one end was attached to the shore.

5 The Fah Machet fortress overlooked Algiers harbor; it consisted of more than a thousand pieces of artillery, of which some eighty guns of various calibers faced the harbor, rendering it a formidable position.

6 The 98-gun HMS *Impregnable*, launched from Chatham in August 1810, was commanded by Admiral David Milne and served as the second flagship during the Battle of Algiers. The ship unintentionally anchored too far away from the lighthouse battery, diminishing the effect of her guns. As a result, the *Impregnable* suffered the heaviest casualties of any British ship during the engagement. The entire fleet suffered a 16 percent casualty rate, making this engagement as bloody as any during the Age of Sail.

7 Edward Brace had a lengthy career in the Royal Navy prior to the attack at Algiers. He won his first naval promotion in 1792, became a captain in 1800, and was knighted in 1834. By the time of his retirement he had advanced to the rank of Vice Admiral of the White.

All our rigging was cut to pieces and the Mizen[8] topmast shot away, and we lay almost becalmed, a perfect wreck, but at 11 pm, we began to haul out, and our boats were sent ahead to tow, and then the Algerines plied us with grape. The *Severn*[9] near us was less crippled than we were, and she got a crowd of sail on her, & she began to draw out, so we made a hawser fast to her Mizen chains, and she towed us out. We anchored out of gunshot at midnight. I was very tired, as we all were, but I was obliged to keep the middle watch, notwithstanding, the proper officer old Walker, having had a contusion somewhere about his precious person, I was right glad to get relieved at 4 o'clock, and I was very deaf from the firing.

On mustering the next morning, we found we had 136 men killed & wounded, out of a complement of 480. The two marine officers were both killed, 2 Lieutenants wounded, 4 Midshipmen killed, & 7 wounded. Thus ended our part of the affair. We were ordered to England immediately and got jury-rigged and made a tolerable passage arriving all safe in England, at Spithead, our Admiral had gone home in the *Glasgow*[10] with Despatches. We were ordered into the harbour, and in passing the platform, an immense crowd had assembled to cheer us. We had 90 round shot in one side, our colours were riddled with grape, and altogether I believe we looked very interesting. The wounded were all sent to the hospital.

We had now a long job before us. The ship required extensive repairs, and we were likely to be some months in the harbour. I was

---

8 The mizenmast is the third, aft-most mast of a three-masted, square-rigged sailing ship.

9 Originally rated to carry 50 guns, HMS *Severn* was commissioned a 40-gun frigate in June 1813. The reduction in armaments was probably because the ship was constructed of pitch-pine—a considerably weaker wood than oak that is less capable of sustaining the weight and stress of additional guns. During the battle at Algiers, three men were killed and thirty-four wounded on the *Severn*, commanded by Captain Frederick William Aylmer.

10 HMS *Glasgow*, completed in February 1814, resembled the *Severn* not only in its pitch-pine construction but also in its reduced armaments: originally a 50-gun frigate, it had been reduced to 40 guns. Captain Anthony Maitland's crew suffered heavy losses in the attack on Algiers: ten men killed and thirty-seven wounded. The *Glasgow* was broken up in January 1829.

appointed Flag Lieutenant to Admiral Milne, who was made a K.C.B.[11] I went home to Drummore on leave of absence, and there I remained three months I think, enjoying myself of course very much. On rejoining, I went in a coach, oh it was tedious work travelling in those days, called the "Highflyer"!! with Sir David Milne, his two sons, David and Alexander,[12] both very fine boys, and their tutor Rev. [Mr.?] Brown, a Presbyterian Minister. The first night we slept at Newcastle, the 2nd night at York, and the 3rd night we travelled all night, reaching London cold & shivering at 6 o'clock in a winter morning.

I joined the ship at Portsmouth, and she was well on in her fitting, and in March we sailed for Bermuda. Arriving there we found Admiral Edward Griffith who we went out to when [manuscript incomplete]

(1817)

FROM BERMUDA WE WENT TO HALIFAX[13] our Head Quarters, the "Admiral's House" not being finished, we had apartments at the Hospital. Lord Dalhousie[14] the Father of the present man, lived at Government house, a fine gentlemanlike soldier & very hospitable. We took him & Lady D on board in the course of the summer, and sailed on a visit to the

---

11 K.C.B. stands for Knight Commander of the Most Honourable Order of the Bath, one of several British orders of chivalry based on the medieval concept of knighthood. Founded in 1725, the Order of the Bath is awarded to members of the armed forces on the recommendation of the prime minister.

12 David and Alexander Milne were sons of Sir David Milne and his first wife, Grace Purves. David, the elder son, would later be one of the founders, and for many years the chairman, of the council of the Scottish Meteorological Society. Alexander followed in his father's footsteps, joining the navy; he ultimately became Admiral of the Fleet.

13 Halifax was the most important and most strongly fortified port and naval base in Nova Scotia, Canada. It is centrally situated on the province's southern coast.

14 George Ramsay was the ninth earl in the peerage of Scotland and the first baron of Dalhousie in the peerage of the United Kingdom. He commanded the seventh British army from 1812 to 1814, fighting on the Spanish peninsula and in France. In 1816, after the defeat of Napoleon, Ramsay was appointed lieutenant governor of Nova Scotia. From 1819 to 1828 he was captain-general and governor-general of Canada, Nova Scotia, New Brunswick, and Prince Edward and Cape Breton Islands. Ramsay served as commander in chief of the East Indies from 1829 to 1832; he died in March 1838.

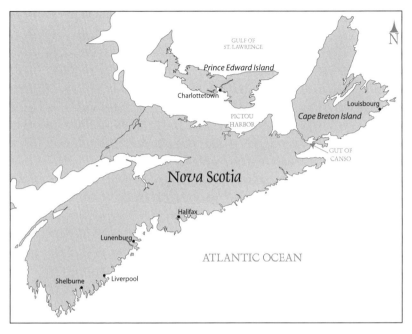

Map of the eastern Canadian coast by Tracy Smith

different sea ports in Nova Scotia, splendid harbours, Liscomb to the Eastward, of Halifax, not settled, the woods adjoining, had been burned down, and there lay the trees, long sticks of charred wood, while other trees, had sprung up in the course of time, and had become when we were there, very respectable trees.

[Margin Note:] There were no Steamboats in this year, in short we had not one in the service. At Halifax a boat, or rather two boats, with paddles between them plied every half hour between Halifax and Dartmouth driven by horses, she was called a Team boat.

Country Harbour, the next harbour to the Eastward not settled, we ran up nine miles from the mouth of it, and anchored, practising at our guns, firing 3 round shot out of every gun, and no chance of hitting any body, there being no inhabitants. It was then a barren land, no trees near, but I believe higher up the Admiral found good fishing. Our next Harbour was Pictou,[15] or rather outside of it, for there was not water enough on the "bar" to allow our ship to cross it. This was then a most flourishing spot. A Mr. Mortimer an early settler and a man of commercial enterprise, was the principal owner of the place, and had built a large stone house, very respectable appearance, and had also planted young trees about it, so as in after days it would have a park like appearance. Nine miles above Pictou, on the East river, coal had just then been found, and when I saw these mines, the seams of coal were very near the surface and 60 feet thick.

We now stood over to Charlotte town,[16] in Prince Edwards Island, and in running in, without a Pilot, by Desbarres'[17] chart (generally very correct). We took the ground but she was soon afloat again. This place was quite in its infancy then, the governor living in a sort of wooden Barracks, and the Island hardly settled. After walking about the place all day, our walks of necessity being very circumscribed, the woods growing close to the town, we were entertained at dinner by the Governor. Our party was large, Lord Dalhousie and his staff and the Admiral with his and we being all very hungry. I think we must have nearly cleaned his larder. The then Governor was a Mr. Smyth,[18] a brother of Sir Sydney.

---

15 Pictou Harbor, an inlet of Northumberland Strait, is a port in Nova Scotia that is closed by ice four months of the year. The port remains an outlet for coal, as Aitchison indicated, as well as for stone.

16 Charlottetown, in the middle part of Prince Edward Island on Hillsborough Bay, is the export center for the island and the seat of the island's fishing industry.

17 Aitchison refers to the portfolio of charts of the northeast coast of North America drawn by cartographer and marine engraver Joseph Frederick Wallet Desbarres. It was published in 1777 for the use of the British navy.

18 Charles Douglas Smith, the oldest son of John Smith and Mary Wilkinson and brother of General Sir William Sydney (or Sidney) Smith, was born in 1763. Joining the army in 1776, Charles Smith served in the North American colonies during the American War for Independence. Because of his brother's influence with Colonial Secretary Lord Bathurst, Lieutenant Colonel Smith received an appointment as governor of Prince Edward Island in August 1812, where he remained until April 1824. He died in February 1855 in Dawlish, England.

I have hitherto omitted to mention Lady Dalhousie,[19] who was also with us, a most unaffected delightful person, a capital sailor, and giving no trouble to anybody. She had then on board also a fine little boy, her youngest son, about 5 years of age, a very manly little fellow. He is now 1858 the present Marquis of Dalhousie, lately Governor General of India.[20]

We now turned our attention to Cape Breton[21] and it was proposed that we should first visit the Lake Brador [Bras d'Or], which was up in the heart of the Island, to within a mile of the passage, leading into the Gut of Canso.[22] I forget the name of that passage, but the *Leander* anchored in the Gut of Canso, and Lord Dalhousie, his staff, the Admiral & myself, went on board the "*Jane*," our Tender, the midshipman of which was the present Lord Hardwicke, then Mr. Yorke.[23] We took one of our cutters in tow, and some Fieldpiece wheels, to mount her on, and drag her into the

---

19 Lady Dalhousie was Christine Broun of Colstoun in Haddingtonshire, the only daughter and heiress of Charles Broun.

20 James Andrew Broun Ramsay, the tenth earl and first marquess of Dalhousie, was the youngest son of George Ramsay. Born in 1812, he accompanied his parents to Canada but returned to England in 1822 to attend school, graduating from Oxford in 1833. Ramsay served in the House of Commons and House of Lords before becoming the governor-general of India, a position he held from 1848 to 1856; at thirty-six he was the youngest man to hold that appointment. Ramsay died at Dalhousie Castle, Scotland, in December 1860.

21 Cape Breton Island, separated from mainland Nova Scotia by the Strait of Canso, was independent of Nova Scotia from 1784 to 1820.

22 The Gut or Strait of Canso is a narrow, deep-water channel—one mile wide and fourteen-and-a-half miles long.

23 Charles Philip Yorke, fourth earl of Hardwicke, from Southampton, joined the navy in 1813. He participated in the British attack on Algiers before being sent to the North American station, where Aitchison encountered him in 1817. Promoted to lieutenant in August 1819, to commander in May 1822, and to captain in June 1825, Yorke represented the connection between the aristocracy and naval establishment under which Aitchison chafed. Although Aitchison joined the navy some five years earlier than Yorke, his promotion to captain trailed Yorke's by two years. Yorke's family connections undoubtedly helped him: he served as a member of Parliament in the early 1830s and became the earl of Hardwicke after the death of his uncle in November 1834. In January 1854 Hardwicke joined the retired list with the rank of rear admiral. He became a retired vice admiral in November 1858 and a retired admiral in December 1863, holding that position until his death in September 1873.

Brador Lake. All this we did very readily and got into her, after she was launched in the Lake, but it was a very uninteresting cruize, and the weather was not fine. The coast on either side was without settlers, and it wore a desolate appearance. We landed at a small chapel, on a point of land, built by the Missionaries (I believe) for the Indians, but none were assembled there at that time. We returned the same way we went & dragged the cutter back. We dined with a Mr. Kavanah at St. Peters, and returned back to the *Leander* next day.

We sailed round to Louisbourg harbour,[24] a spot famous formerly when in possession of the French, but after it was taken from them, the works were destroyed, and all that remains now are mounds of green banks, and a few Fishermans huts and settlers remain, where the town stood. It was here that a very ludicrous act was performed by Dick Baird, one of our Midshipmen. Dick was a good natured rollicking sort of chap, about 17, a son of Sir J[ohn] B[aird], but he began to be very fond of a glass of grog. The Midshipmen, his messmates, made Dick the caterer, which he did not much fancy, but when fairly installed he was obliged to perform his duties, and his messmates furnished him with funds to go on shore and buy some fresh stock. Dick was all abroad, he did not know what to buy, but it all at once occurred to him, if he were to buy a Bullock, it would save him a great deal of trouble, and he could salt the meat for the mess, as much as they did not consume fresh. So he bought a bullock, and then a difficulty arose in Dick's mind, how he was to get him on board the ship, a mile off. He had one of the cutters with him, so there was nothing left for it but to make the poor brute take to the water and swim him off. Accordingly he managed to get him into deep water, and he took him in tow, by the horns. By this time, it was drawing towards sunset,

---

24 Louisbourg on Cape Breton Island was a strongly fortified port founded by the French in 1713. Its location permitted the French to maintain strategic control over the entrance to the Gulf of St. Lawrence. During the War of Austrian Succession (King George's War) it was besieged and captured by American colonials led by Sir William Pepperell; the 1748 Treaty of Aix-la-Chapelle returned the fort to the French. In 1758, during the Seven Years' War (French and Indian War), British general Jeffrey Amherst and Admiral Edward Boscawen captured the bastion and soon thereafter destroyed the fortifications.

when the cutter ought to have been off. At length she was seen from the ship, coming off very slowly. The First Lieutenant became impatient, hoisted the signal of recall to the cutter, but it was of no use, she could come no faster. At last we saw she had something in tow, and as she approached, we saw the horns of Dick's victim astern, and every thing was got ready to hoist it on board by the horns. Up came Dick, "I have come on board, Sir" to the First Lieutenant. What have you got there, Mr. Baird, said the Captain, looking very grave. "Sea stock, Sir, for the Midshipmens Berth" answered Dick, looking as if he did not look upon it as a joke at all. His messmates had all come on deck to see the upshot of it, which was that the Captain was very angry with poor Dick, and he ordered the Purser to take the Bullock off his hands, to pay him what he paid for it, and serve it out to the Ship's company. Dick's office of Caterer, of course, did not survive this, and his messmates were obliged to supersede him, to his great joy. Poor Dick fell into a consumption and died in Bermuda Hospital in July 1819.

We visited other ports of Nova Scotia to the westward by Lunenberg, Liverpool & Shelburn.[25] Liverpool was very thriving place, with a good trade to the West Indies. Shelburne had quite gone to decay, a fine harbour but barren land.

In December, we went to Bermuda for the winter. A snow storm caught us before we left Halifax, and running down to Bermuda we had a gale of wind, and sprang the Fore Yard.[26] At Bermuda, the Admiral hired Mount Wyndham in preference to living at St. Johns house, on Spanish Point. It was a beautiful situation, standing on a hill above Baillies Bay,[27] and about a mile & a half from St. Georges Ferry. I lived on

---

25 Lunenburg (some thirty-seven miles southwest of Halifax) and Liverpool (an additional thirty-seven miles down the coast) were two of Canada's most important fishing centers. Shelburne, even further to the southwest, was a major port and shipbuilding facility founded in 1783 by loyalists from the United States.

26 When Aitchison remarks that wind sprang the foreyard, he was most likely referring to the spar that holds the foresail or forecourse, the principal and lowest sail on the foremast.

27 Bailey's Bay, site of several of Bermuda's most spectacular caves, sits on the eastern tip of Hamilton Parish.

Map of Bermuda by Tracy Smith

shore with the Admiral. We had the Band, a guard, and a boats crew, all
lodged up there, and a very unruly set they were. *(1818)* Then there
was the Secretary, Mr. L'Amy, Mr. Brown the Tutor, and the two boys. viz.
Mr. Milne home now,[28] and Admiral Alex Milne 1858. We used to play
whist[29] every night, and the Admiral & I played Quoits[30] in the day. The
Governor Sir James Cockburn,[31] dined once a week with us, and we dined
with him once a week, and thus we whiled away the winter.

The Caves near where we lived attracted us often to them. Some
of them ran a great depth, and generally had a quantity of salt water in
them, and the roofs were beautifully furnished with stalactites, and the
floor of these caves had sometimes pillars, which were formed by drop-
pings from the roof, and they had a beautiful appearance when lighted
up. The Admiral got permission to remove many of these stalactites, and
one which ran from the centre of Tuckers Cave, we removed, and took
home with us, and it now is to be seen in the College Museum at
Edin[burgh] along with many others. The large one, I had a good deal
to do with, in getting it out of the cave. It weighed about 5 tons, and we
had to make a road for it, in the cave for near 100 yards. We took some

fine specimens of Madrepore[32] to Edin[burgh] also. They form at the bottom of the sea, some of them deeply indented, and they give them the name of "Brain Stones." I think some of those the Admiral took home must have been 3 feet in diameter. The way we got them up from the bottom was simply this, the water being quite transparent, you could detect them 7 fathoms under water, but those we brought up, perhaps were not as many feet under. We had a strong net made, which was let down along the side the stone you wished to take, and then with a boat hook, you detached it easily from the bottom and then turned it into the net.

At Mount Wyndham, we were supplied with water almost entirely from our Tank, which would have been quite ample to have supplied an ordinary establishment, but with our large numbers, we were occasionally obliged to bring water up to the top of the hill in casks. There are no springs in Bermuda. The whole Island depends on rain water, so sometimes they are short off.

Bermuda is entirely calcareous. The stones with which they build their homes, are sawed up, but the stone hardens by exposure to the air. The soil in the valley is rich, the Island is covered nearly with Cedar trees. The houses are built of Cedar, the fire wood is Cedar, vessels are built of Cedar, every thing smells of Cedar, and indeed you can smell the Islands, almost before you sight them.

The Native boats are very handy, two sails generally, the breadth of the boat <u>one</u> <u>half</u> the <u>length</u> of the <u>keel</u>, the mast <u>twice</u> the length of the keel. They sail within 4 points of the wind, the sails standing like boards.

We had during the war which ended in 1814 several men of war schooners built of cedar at Bermuda. The wood is very durable, but heavy.

---

28 David, the elder Milne son, adopted the surname Milne-Home after his marriage to the heiress Jean Foreman-Home.

29 Whist is a card game resembling bridge that is usually played by two pairs of players.

30 Quoits is a game in which rings are thrown at a peg.

31 James Cockburn, the older brother of Admiral George Cockburn, served as governor of Bermuda from 1811 to 1819.

32 Madrepore, or brain stones, are stony, often round, brain-shaped corals of the genus *Acropora*. The term "madrepore" is often applied to any stony coral.

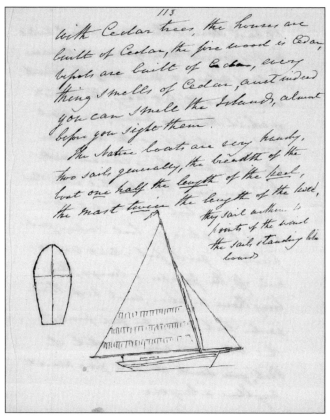

Sketch of native boat, profile and bottom

The Islands of which there are many are most enchanting to look at, the houses are all white, and being covered with these ever green trees, <u>peopled</u> with Red & Blue birds, look very cheerful. It is a capital place for boat sailing, and plenty of good fish, about 8 or 10 miles off, the Grouper & Porgy, they bring them in alive, and keep them under lock & key, in fish ponds, so that when you want a dish of Fish, you send down to your nearest neighbour & buy one.

In the Month of March, Whales make their appearance off the Islands on their way to the Northward, and then begins the busy time, with the negroes. They often take a good many of them, and looking from Mount Wyndham with a good glass, you could see them in full pursuit. The Negroes get quite fat, during this season, they eat quantities of whale, and it is by no means bad, a piece of a young whale eats like coarse beef.

[Margin note:] The Negroes were a lazy set but of course they are now emancipated.

We generally quitted Bermuda about May and went up to Halifax, the weather then becoming hot, the Yellow Fever which has appeared at Bermuda periodically of late years was hardly known at that time then.

(1819)

IN JUNE 1819 WE WERE RELIEVED by Admiral Griffith with his Flag in the *Newcastle*,[33] Captain Fanshaw,[34] and to our great joy we sailed for England and arrived in July and were paid off. I received my Commission[35] when the Admiral hauled his Flag down as Commander and then I went home and remained nearly 8 years on half pay without interest enough to get a ship at length.

(1826)

I WAS IN 1826 in April appointed to command the *Clio*[36] at Chatham an 18-gun Brig and in three months we were ready for Sea which was a

---

33 HMS *Newcastle*, a 60-gun frigate built of pitch pine and launched in November 1813, carried a combination of cannons and carronades. Her soft-wood construction, combined with an infestation of teredo worms from the West Indies, reduced her effectiveness. She was converted to harbor service in June 1824 and sold in June 1850.

34 Arthur Fanshawe was promoted to captain in October 1816 and shortly thereafter gained command of the *Newcastle*; he had been promoted from lieutenant, to commander, to captain in less than four years. Although Fanshawe climbed the lower ranks quickly, he never became an admiral.

35 The commission to which Aitchison is referring is his promotion to the rank of commander; the commission was dated July 17, 1819.

36 HMS *Clio* was an 18-gun brig-sloop launched from Mistleythorn in January 1807. As commander of the ship, from 1826 to 1827, Aitchison defended it against smugglers in the North Sea; the *Clio* was broken up in March 1845.

long time but what with Dock yard delays and a difficulty in getting men for the home station we could make but little progress.

I sailed for Leith on the 29th June having received my orders from Sir Robert Moorsom[37] the Commander in chief at Chatham which was to cruize for the suppression of smuggling between the Shetland Islands and North Foreland a pretty long stretch. I called at Yarmouth, at Shields and off Holy Island and landed at the old Bamborough Castle with the youngsters to show them it. There was an apparatus kept there to assist in saving the lives of Shipwrecked Mariners and as the Castle belonged to the Bishopries of Durham some of the Church occupied it during the summer months. We found there a most hospitable man, one of the Prebendaries[38] of Durham, Mr. [Damwell?] and he gave us a most sumptuous luncheon. It was quite unexpected on my part because I thought of seeing only an old Artillery Sergeant or some such person and I was very much horrified when I saw these Midshipmen devouring the many tarts and pies in the way they did.

I stayed at Leith only a few days and then sailed for Shetland making the Islands about 2 am then—almost—broad daylight. My North Sea Pilot ran us up to Lerwick[39] where we came to an anchor close off the Town, which is a miserable little place with a small Fort there for its protection.

Got Shetland Ponies and rode out to Scalloway Castle. It is quite a ruin now and the beach about it is used as curing ground by the Fishermen in the locality.

---

37 Robert Moorsom gained his first naval promotion in January 1784 and by August 1811 had become Rear Admiral of the White. From 1812 to 1820 he served as a member of Parliament from Queensborough. Moorsom eventually reached the rank of Admiral of the Blue and was knighted. He died in May 1835.

38 A prebendary is a member of the clergy entitled to a stipend allotted from the revenues of a cathedral.

39 Lerwick, a fishing burgh in Aitchison's time, has since become the Shetland Islands' largest town and administrative center. It is located on the eastern shore of Mainland Island, the largest of the Shetland group. The Shetland Islands, the northernmost islands of Great Britain, lie approximately 130 miles north of the Scottish coast.

[The following text appears on one unnumbered, folded loose-leaf page, dated Mapperton[40] July 6-60.]

I was cruizing off Flamborough Head[41] in the Month of March 1827 in search of smugglers and it had been blowing strong from the N.W. so that we were under snug sail, treble reefed topsails, foresail, trysail, Top gallant yards on deck & masts [illegible]. At daylight we were standing in shore and I was looking round with my glass when I saw a lugger about 4 miles on our lee bow with his trysails set, and head in the same way as ours. I asked old [Payne?], our North Sea Pilot, what he thought of her, and after due examination he pronounced her a Yorkshire cable laying his lines. I thought otherwise & made preparation for the chase. It was blowing fresh still but I determined to shake out two reefs and clap every stitch of sail on the Brig at once. We quietly shifted the trysail,[42] set the lower mainsail & jib and made all ready to out reefs and run up the Top gallant-masts & yards and up helm and after him. He was watching us like a cat. The hands were turned up "make all sail in chase" and we bore up & flew through the water. No sooner than this measure was performed then our friend did the same, down trysail and up with his whacking jib[43] and luge lugs[44] and way before the wind. No doubt now of his nature, we did not gain much upon him but still we gradually [wore?] him until the breeze "took off" and then he held his own. The young ones now

---

40 Aitchison resided in Mapperton, Dorset, late in life.

41 Flamborough Head is a promontory on the eastern coast of Yorkshire in northern England. At some 214 feet above the water level, Flamborough Head is known for chalky cliffs and abundant caverns.

42 A trysail is a small triangular sail that is usually set when heaving to in a gale. "Heaving to" is a precautionary measure in which shortened and trimmed sails work in concert with steering to keep a vessel's bow pointing up into the wind, thus reducing drift and roll in heavy seas.

43 Jibs are triangular sails set on the stays of the foremast. Large sailing ships might carry as many as six jibs, whereas smaller vessels might set but one. A whacking jib is an informal description of a very large jib.

44 The term "luge lugs" refers to the pole-like yards on which a lugsail is hoisted. A lugsail is a four-sided sail used mainly on small craft; vessels carrying such sails are often called "luggers."

A View of His Majesty's Dock Yard at Chatham in the County of Kent, on the River Medway, *engraving by Carington Bowles after John Clevely, Jr., London, 1772. Courtesy of the Naval Historical Center. Chatham Dockyard emerged as a major shipbuilding center in the sixteenth century and remained in operation for some four hundred years, closing on March 31, 1984. Aitchison's uncle, the eminent engineer John Rennie, was responsible for major dockyard improvements in the early nineteenth century.*

Vue du Chantier de Sa Majesté à CHATHAM, dans le Comté de KENT, sur la Riviere Medway.

LONDON. Published as the Act directs 1.st Jan.y 1771.

were anxious to have at him with the boats and I had some little difficulty in suppressing their anxiety, but we had the two galleys all ready to
lower the moment the breeze failed, which it soon did, and away went
the second Lieutenant in charge of the two beautiful boats. The smuggler,
for such she was, out sweeps[45] and made good work of it. We were now
becalmed. The smugglers pulling for their lives drew the boats soon out
of sight from the deck, but they were coming up with her just when an
ominous Fog bank appeared in the S.E. (to seaward). Out of this came a
breeze and we soon saw the chase on the starboard tack with a freshen-
ing wind. I made the signal of recall, boats out of sight, weather getting
thick, the day wearing fast away and I confess that I was painfully anxious for their fate.

[After several dozen blank pages, Aitchison inserts line sketches of three
single-mast boats with lateen sails.]

---

45 When pursuing or pursued, smaller sailing vessels could "out sweeps"—or use long
oars—if the wind failed.

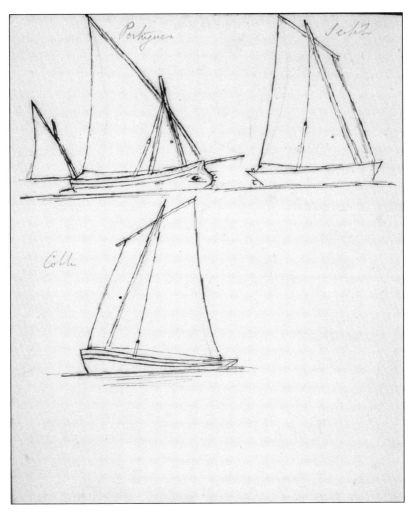

"Portuguese," "Scotch," and "Coble"

CONCLUSION

ROBERT AITCHISON'S CAREER in the Royal Navy mirrored that of many British officers in the early nineteenth century. The wars against France and the United States, followed by the attack on the North African port of Algiers, provided Aitchison occasion to advance within the navy. Yet once the wars concluded, Aitchison's professional usefulness, like that of many other young officers, quickly came to an end. The navy began demobilizing its ships and dismissing its sizable corps of sailors and officers. The period from 1814 to 1864, known as the "Great Slump," hit the commissioned officer corps extremely hard.[1]

Aitchison's postwar career serves as a poignant example of the troubles facing individuals and the navy during the Great Slump. The Royal Navy had grown considerably during the late war years (1808-1813)— years that correspond with Aitchison's early service. Unfortunately, Aitchison did not win his officer's commission during this growth period; his lieutenancy was confirmed in May 1815, when the navy had already started to demobilize. In the years between 1813 and 1818, the size of the navy shrank dramatically—the number of ships fell from 899 to 555, the number of sailors from 140,000 to 20,000. Yet during the same period the number of active[2] commissioned officers increased from 4,873 to 5,797. The result was, of course, too few ships for too many officers. By 1818, almost 90 percent of British officers were on the navy's unemployed list.[3]

Aitchison avoided joining the ranks of the unemployed in the immediate aftermath of the Napoleonic Wars. He served aboard HMS *Leander* in her celebrated August 1816 bombardment of Algiers and after-

---

1 Michael Lewis, *The Navy in Transition, 1814-1864: A Social History* (London, 1965), 47-48.
2 The term "active" excludes retired and superannuated officers but does not imply "active" employment.
3 Lewis, *Navy in Transition*, 64-69; O'Byrne, *Naval Biographical Dictionary*, 7.

wards spent three years as Admiral Sir David Milne's flag lieutenant on the North American station, as recounted in the latter part of the memoir. Aitchison's close connection to Milne afforded him greater career opportunities than many of his peers. In fact, Aitchison was lucky—of more than 4,000 lieutenants on the navy list in 1818, only 449, or 11.1 percent, saw active service. By July 1819 Aitchison had been promoted to the rank of commander—a position he held for the next eight years—and suddenly he, too, began to suffer the consequences of the swollen officer corps. In 1824 there were 923 commanders on the navy list, yet only 64, or 7.9 percent, had active appointments. Aitchison remained on the unemployed list until April 1826, when he gained command of the 18-gun brig sloop *Clio*, which the navy used to fight smuggling in the North Sea.[4]

Officers in the lower ranks were forced to compete to get the attention of the selection boards that awarded promotions and assignments. A fortunate junior officer might gain quick promotion through heroic acts, dutiful service, or personal associations—but many of the less fortunate remained midshipmen, lieutenants, or commanders until their deaths. Once a lucky officer "made post"—or won promotion to captain—all further advancement was based solely on seniority. To advance past the rank of captain, it was necessary for a more senior officer either to die or retire. When Aitchison made post in April 1827, he immediately proceeded to the bottom of a seniority list that had more than 800 captains in 1832 and more than 750 in 1842. Little hope remained of his ever seeing active service again or reaching the rank of admiral. The Admiralty Office had simply promoted too many men during the war period.[5]

Many British naval officers chose not to wait until they were old men for promotions or ship commands. Some offered their services to foreign causes, including the Latin American revolutionaries trying to secure their independence from Spain, the Brazilian government strug-

---

4 O'Byrne, *Naval Biographical Dictionary*, 7; Lewis, *Navy in Transition*, 84, 87.

5 O'Byrne, *Naval Biographical Dictionary*, 7; Basil Greenhill and Ann Giffard, *Steam, Politics and Patronage: The Transformation of the Royal Navy, 1815-54* (London, 1994), 59-60; Lewis, *Navy in Transition*, 50-51, 78; PRO, ADM 9/18, folio 24.

gling against Portugal, and the Greeks waging a war of independence against Turkey. Robert Aitchison did not choose to join a foreign navy. Instead, he remained on half pay from the time of his promotion in 1827 until his retirement in 1849. All told, he spent twenty-two years—or more than half of his naval career—on half pay. By the time he retired, the fifty-three-year-old Aitchison had not climbed the promotional ladder high enough to anticipate promotion to flag rank (or admiral). Captains Robert Lambert Baynes and Thomas Bennett, Aitchison's peers, secured their post commands in 1828 and received their flags in 1855, almost twenty-seven years later. Neither would have secured promotion to flag rank without the retirement of many officers above him on the promotional ladder.[6]

Rather than wait for a promotion that might never come to pass, Aitchison retired and began collecting £356 per year in retirement pay. And, although retired, he continued a slow climb up the navy's hierarchical ladder. The Admiralty Office awarded honorary post-retirement promotions to those individuals who had spent much of their careers in their respective ranks; by providing an incentive to retire, these promotions helped relieve competition on the active service list. Aitchison won promotion to retired rear admiral in August 1854, with the pay—slightly more than £456 per year—of a retired captain. Aitchison now stood eighty-ninth on the list of retired admirals. Had he lived long enough, he might have reached the rank of retired vice admiral or even retired admiral—ranks he never would have secured while in active service.[7]

More so than many of his peers in the navy, who struggled to find the means to supplement their meager earnings, Aitchison remained shielded from financial strain. His father, William, had amassed extensive land holdings, including the five-hundred-acre Drummore estate in

---

6 See, for instance, Peter McCormick, "The Improbable Thomas Cochrane," *Military History Quarterly* 8 (Spring 1996): 100; Brian Vale, *Independence or Death! British Sailors and Brazilian Independence, 1822-25* (London, 1996), 20-22, 30; and *The Navy List*, accessed via Paul Benyon, *Index to 19th and Early 20th Century Naval and Naval Social History*, http://www.pbenyon.plus.com/Nbd/Index.html.

7 O'Byrne, *Naval Biographical Dictionary*, 7; Lewis, *Navy in Transition*, 79-80; *The Navy List: 1856* (London, 1856), 217.

Musselburgh and the Bordland property in Spittalhaugh; William also engaged in real estate speculation, renovating and reselling the Queensberry House, a seventeenth-century dwelling on the present-day site of the Scottish Parliament. Drummore devolved to the eldest son, William, who ranked as one of the "chief proprietors" in the parish of Prestonpans. Bordland, meanwhile, passed in trust to all seven brothers, who deeded the property to Francis in 1840. By all indications, the Aitchison siblings were deeply attached to one another; historian W. F. K. Thompson, who edited John's letters for publication, has described them as "a close-knit family much concerned with each other's welfare." Had family members considered Robert a needy case, they would have had the means to provide for him. Thus, although few details of Robert's personal finances are known, it seems unlikely that he suffered the privations of other officers stranded at half pay.[8]

Those of Robert's records that do exist paint a picture of relative prosperity and domestic contentment. In 1821 Robert married Eliza Munro, daughter of Matthew Munro, Esquire, from the Caribbean island of Grenada. Since most English families with property in the Caribbean chose to spend only part of the year—generally winter—in the islands, it is likely that the December wedding of Eliza and Robert represented a gala affair for both families.[9]

By 1830 the Aitchisons resided in Eling, a fishing village across the bay from Southampton, England. Robert had secured an appointment as a justice for Hampshire County, a position that gave him the use of a dwelling house and adjacent buildings. The salary from this position, combined with his naval half pay, must have significantly eased any finan-

---

8 "William Aitchison (1784-1837)," *The Usher Family of Scotland*, http://freepages .genealogy.rootsweb.com/~usher/ushersct/4009.htm; Thomas Addyman, William Kay, and Shelly Brown, "Queensberry House," *The Holyrood Archaeology Project: The Scottish Parliament Excavation*, http://www .holyroodarchaeology.org/queen.html; "Statistical Account of Scotland 1845: Parish of Prestonpans," Prestonpans Historical Society, http://www.prestoungrange.org/prestonpans/ html/accounts_1845/1.html; Thompson, introduction to *An Ensign in the Peninsular War*, 9.
9 O'Byrne, *Naval Biographical Dictionary*, 7.

cial concerns he may have had at this period. The appointment also paid social dividends, bringing Robert into contact with local community leaders. One, Henry Combe Compton (1789-1866) of Minstead Manor House, would come to play a significant role in Robert's life. Compton served in Parliament for South Hampshire from 1835 to 1857 and also held the position of verderer—an officer instructed to administer and to preserve the flora and fauna—for the New Forest, a royal deer-hunting enclave and woodland.[10]

Although the record books remain incomplete, Eliza died sometime before 1838—for in April of that year Robert was remarried, to Compton's daughter Lucretia Catherine. Over the next thirteen years the couple had four children. Son Henry Compton, born in 1844 in New Forest, followed his father into the navy, where by the time of his death in September 1891 he had attained the rank of rear admiral. Daughter Jane Charlotte was born in New Forest in 1842, while daughters Lucretia Catherine (1845) and Selina (1850 or 1851) were born in Dorset. The Aitchisons apparently lived in moderate comfort, if not extravagance; they resided for part of their marriage at Shrubs Hill House in the village of Lyndhurst and attended nearby St. Michael and All Angel's Church, where Mrs. Aitchison's relative John Compton served as rector. A pair of Pre-Raphaelite stained glass windows in the church bears witness to the family's presence in the region—the East Window memorializes Robert

---

10 "Justice Robert Aitchison esq.; Property, Messuages and land at Eling," Hampshire Record Office, Hampshire Quarter Sessions, c. 1350-1970, Q 27/3/281, 1830, http://www.a2a.org.uk/; "Southampton—Sir Henry Charles Paulet to replace Henry Combe Compton as verderer for the New Forest," PRO, Petty Bag Office: Writ Files, C 202/256/19, http://www.combs-families.org/combs/records/england/pro/c.htm; "Minstead Parish Council: History," *New Forest District Council*, http://www .nfdc.gov.uk/index.cfm?Articleid=2364; Michael Stenton, *Who's Who of British Members of Parliament: A Biographical Dictionary of the House of Commons Based on Annual Volumes of Dod's Parliamentary Companion and Other Sources*, vol. 1, 1832-1855 (Atlantic Highlands, NJ, 1976), 88.

and his middle daughter, while the West Window memorializes son Henry and daughter-in-law Constance Fanny.[11]

By 1851 the Aitchisons resided in Mapperton, Dorset—and when Aitchison commenced his memoir he jotted "Brussels" and the date "1857" on the manuscript. The family may have chosen to live abroad where Robert's salary could stretch further; the cost of living on the continent was considerably cheaper than the cost of living in England. The notation could also indicate that Aitchison and his family were on holiday in Belgium. Both possibilities seem plausible, and the latter could explain why the manuscript remains incomplete—once the vacation ended and the family returned to England, Aitchison could have become preoccupied with domestic matters. A single loose-leaf page, tucked into the journal and dated July 1860, indicates one final attempt to pick up the thread of the narrative.

Robert Aitchison's trail fades away at this point. We know that he died on February 13, 1861, at the age of sixty-five.[12] And we know that, in a twist of fate, his widow remarried Admiral Sir Henry John Codrington, the son of Robert Aitchison's commander at the Battle of New Orleans; in January 1877, just months before his death, Sir Henry became Admiral of the Fleet—the highest ranking office in the British Navy.[13]

While Robert Aitchison did not rise to the top of the naval profession nor become distinguished in another field, he has finally gained the

---

11 O'Byrne, *Naval Biographical Dictionary*, 7; Aitchison family correspondence in the possession of Helen Mound; "St Michaels and All Angels: Lyndhurst," *Southern Life (UK)*, http://freepages.genealogy.rootsweb.com/~villages/lyndchur.htm; National Maritime Museum, "Memorial M3071" and "Memorial M3072," *Maritime Memorials: Commemorating Seafarers and Victims of Maritime Disasters*, http://www.nmm.ac.uk/memorials/Memorial.cfm?Search=aitchison&SearchCriteria=Surname&Area=&MemorialID=M3071 and http://www.nmm.ac.uk/memorials/Memorial.cfm?Search=aitchison&SearchCriteria=Surname&Area=&MemorialID=M3072.

12 While Robert lived a reasonably long life by nineteenth-century standards, his lifespan was only average for his family. Robert's mother, sister, and two of his brothers also reached their sixties. His father lived to be 85; and brothers David (76 or 77), John (85 or 86), and James (a remarkable 99) were quite long-lived.

Aitchison family memorial, Inveresk Kirkyard, Scotland. Robert's parents, sister, and brothers George and William are buried here. Photograph courtesy of George McLeod, Midlothian Historical Society, Scotland

recognition he deserves. His unfinished memoir offers readers a glimpse of the bygone "Age of Sail"—a time in which the British navy dominated the seas. Aitchison provides insights into the relationships that developed among officers as they struggled to survive the crucible of war. He also depicts the often mundane life of a young officer's coming-of-age during the struggle with France, the United States, and Algiers. Yet equally

---

13 O'Byrne, *Naval Biographical Dictionary*, 7; PRO, ADM 9/18, folio 24; *Navy List: 1856*, 217; National Maritime Museum, "Memorial 3071"; Nigel Batty-Smith, "Admiral of the Fleet Sir Henry John Codrington K.C.B.," *United Kingdom Genealogy*, http://www.uk-genealogy.org.uk/Database/D0020/I9241.html; "Person Page 1807," *ThePeerage.com: A Genealogical Survey of the Peerage of Britain as Well as the Royal Families of Europe*, http://www.thepeerage.com/p1807.htm.

important are his descriptions of exotic locations that he visited and the unusual flora and fauna he encountered. Aitchison's memoir is a valuable addition to the published material on the Royal Navy and its role in the War of 1812, especially during the Battle of New Orleans. Robert Aitchison's eyewitness account offers us a unique perspective on this critical moment in American history.

BIBLIOGRAPHY

ARCHIVAL SOURCES

Aitchison family history and correspondence in the possession of Helen Mound, Worcestershire, UK.

Robert Aitchison memoir. The Historic New Orleans Collection.

United Kingdom. Public Record Office. Admiralty: Survey Returns of Officers' Services, 1817-1848. The National Archives, Kew, London.

ADDITIONAL PRIMARY SOURCES

Aitchison, John. *An Ensign in the Peninsular War: The Letters of John Aitchison*. Ed. W. F. K. Thompson. London: Michael Joseph, 1981.

Cooke, John Henry. *A Narrative of Events in the South of France, and of the Attack on New Orleans, in 1814 and 1815*. London: T. & W. Boone, 1835.

Davison, Gideon M., and Samuel Williams. *Sketches of the War, between the United States and the British Isles*. Rutland, VT: Fay and Davison, 1815.

Dudley, William S., ed. *The Naval War of 1812: A Documentary History*. 3 vols. to date. Washington, DC: Naval Historical Center, Dept. of Navy, 1985–.

Dunlop, William. *Recollections of the American War, 1812-14*. Toronto: Historical Publishing Co., 1905.

Gleig, George Robert. *A Narrative of the Campaigns of the British Army at Washington and New Orleans, under Generals Ross, Pakenham and Lambert . . . .* London: John Murray, 1821.

Hill, Benson E. *Recollections of an Artillery Officer: Including Scenes and Adventures in Ireland, America, Flanders and France*. 2 vols. London: Richard Bentley, 1836.

James, William. *A Full and Correct Account of the Military Occurrences of the Late War between Great Britain and the United States of America . . . .* London: Printed for the author, 1818.

Latour, Arsène Lacarrière. *Historical Memoir of the War in West Florida and Louisiana in 1814-15, with an Atlas*. Edited by Gene A. Smith. Gainesville: University Press of Florida in association with The Historic New Orleans Collection, 1999.

Le Couteur, John. *Merry Hearts Make Light Days: The War of 1812 Journal of Lieutenant John Le Couteur, 104th Foot*. Edited by Donald E. Graves. Ottawa: Carleton University Press, 1993.

Mullins, Thomas. *General Court Martial Held, at the Royal Barracks, Dublin, for the Trial of Brevet Lieutenant-Colonel Hon. Thomas Mullins . . . .* Dublin: William Epsy, 1815.

Norton, John. *The Journal of Major John Norton.* Edited by Carl F. Klinck and James J. Talman. Toronto: Champlain Society, 1970.

Pringle, Norman P. *Letters by Major Norman Pringle, Late of the 21st Royal Scots Fusileers, Vindicating the Character of the British Army Employed in North America in the Years 1814-15 . . . .* [Edinburgh?]: 1834.

Richardson, James D., ed. *A Compilation of the Messages and Papers of the Presidents, 1789-1897.* Vol. 1, 1789-1817. Washington, DC: Government Printing Office, 1896.

United Kingdom. H. M. Stationery Office. *The Navy List,* 1808-1861.

SECONDARY SOURCES

Carter, Samuel. *Blaze of Glory: The Fight for New Orleans, 1814-1815.* New York: St. Martin's Press, 1971.

Clowes, William Laird, et al. *The Royal Navy: A History from the Earliest Times to the Present.* 7 vols. Boston: Little, Brown and Co., 1897-1901.

Colledge, J. J. *Ships of the Royal Navy.* 2 vols. Annapolis: Naval Institute Press, 1987-89.

Fortescue, J. W. *A History of the British Army.* 13 vols. London: Macmillan, 1899-1930.

Greenhill, Basil, and Ann Giffard. *Steam, Politics and Patronage: The Transformation of the Royal Navy, 1815-54.* London: Conway Maritime Press, 1994.

Hacker, Louis M. "Western Land Hunger and the War of 1812: A Conjecture." *Mississippi Valley Historical Review* 10 (March 1924): 365-95.

Hill, J. R., ed. *The Oxford Illustrated History of the Royal Navy.* Oxford: Oxford University Press, 1995.

Hill, Richard. *The Prizes of War: The Naval Prize System in the Napoleonic Wars, 1793-1815.* Portsmouth, UK: Royal Naval Museum Publications, 1998.

Horsman, Reginald. "British Indian Policy in the Northwest, 1807-1812." *Mississippi Valley Historical Review* 45 (June 1958): 51-66.

_____. *The Causes of the War of 1812.* Philadelphia: University of Pennsylvania Press, 1962.

_____. "Western War Aims, 1811-1812." *Indiana Magazine of History* 53 (March 1957): 1-18.

Ireland, Bernard. *Naval Warfare in the Age of Sail*. New York: Norton, 2000.

Kemp, Peter. *The British Sailor: A Social History of the Lower Deck*. London: Dent, 1970.

King, Dean, John B. Hattendorf, and J. Worth Estes. *A Sea of Words: A Lexicon and Companion for Patrick O'Brian's Seafaring Tales*. New York: Henry Holt, 2000.

Lambert, Andrew D. *War at Sea in the Age of Sail: 1650-1850*. London: Cassell, 2000.

Latimer, Margaret K. "South Carolina—A Protagonist of the War of 1812." *American Historical Review* 61 (July 1956): 914-29.

Lavery, Brian. *Nelson's Navy: The Ships, Men and Organisation, 1793-1815*. Annapolis: Naval Institute Press, 1989.

Lewis, Michael. *The Navy in Transition, 1814-1864: A Social History*. London: Hodder and Stoughton, 1965.

————. *A Social History of the Navy, 1793-1815*. London: Allen and Unwin, 1960.

Mahan, Alfred Thayer. *The Influence of Sea Power upon the French Revolution and Empire, 1793-1812*. Boston: Little, Brown and Co., 1898.

————. *Sea Power in Its Relations to the War of 1812*. 1905. Reprint, New York: Haskell House, 1969.

McCormick, Peter. "The Improbable Thomas Cochrane." *Military History Quarterly* 8 (Spring 1996): 94-101.

Miller, Nathan. *Broadsides: The Age of Fighting Sail, 1775-1815*. New York: Wiley, 2000.

Morriss, Roger. *Cockburn and the British Navy in Transition: Admiral Sir George Cockburn, 1772-1853*. Columbia: University of South Carolina Press, 1997.

A Naval Encyclopædia: Comprising a Dictionary of Nautical Words and Phrases . . . . Philadephia: L. R. Hamersly and Co., 1881.

O'Byrne, William R., ed. *A Naval Biographical Dictionary: Comprising the Life and Services of Every Living Officer in Her Majesty's Navy, from the Rank of Admiral of the Fleet to that of Lieutenant, Inclusive*. London: J. Murray, 1849.

Oman, Charles William Chadwick. *Wellington's Army, 1809-1814*. London: E. Arnold, 1913.

Owsley, Frank L., Jr., and Gene A. Smith. *Filibusters and Expansionists: Jeffersonian Manifest Destiny, 1800-1821*. Tuscaloosa: University of Alabama Press, 1997.

Pack, James. *The Man Who Burned the White House: Admiral Sir George Cockburn, 1772-1853*. Annapolis: Naval Institute Press, 1987.

Perkins, Bradford. *Prologue to War: England and the United States, 1805-1812*. Berkeley: University of California Press, 1961.

_____, ed. *The Causes of the War of 1812: National Honor or National Interest?* New York: Holt, Rinehart and Winston, 1962.

Pivka, Otto von. *Navies of the Napoleonic Era.* New York: Hippocrene Books, 1980.

Pratt, Julius. "Western Aims in the War of 1812." *Mississippi Valley Historical Review* 12 (June 1925): 36-50.

Roosevelt, Theodore. *The Naval War of 1812.* 1882. Reprint, Annapolis: Naval Institute Press, 1987.

Smith, Gene A. *Thomas ap Catesby Jones: Commodore of Manifest Destiny.* Annapolis: Naval Institute Press, 2000.

Spicer, Stanley. *The Age of Sail: The Master Shipbuilders of the Maritimes.* Halifax: Formac, 2001.

Stenton, Michael. *Who's Who of British Members of Parliament: A Biographical Dictionary of the House of Commons Based on Annual Volumes of Dod's Parliamentary Companion and Other Sources.* Vol. 1, 1832-1885. Atlantic Highlands, NJ: Humanities Press, 1976.

Tucker, Spencer C., and Frank T. Reuter. *Injured Honor: The Chesapeake-Leopard Affair, June 22, 1807.* Annapolis: Naval Institute Press, 1996.

Vale, Brian. *Independence or Death! British Sailors and Brazilian Independence, 1822-25.* London: I. B. Tauris, 1996.

ELECTRONIC SOURCES

Addyman, Thomas, William Kay, and Shelly Brown. "Queensberry House." *The Holyrood Archaeology Project: The Scottish Parliament Excavation.* http://www.holyroodarchaeology.org/queen.html.

Batty-Smith, Nigel. "Admiral of the Fleet Sir Henry John Codrington K.C.B." *United Kingdom Genealogy.* http://www.ukgenealogy.org.uk/Database/D0020/I9241.html.

Benyon, Paul. *Index to 19th and Early 20th Century Naval and Naval Social History.* http://www.pbenyon.plus.com/Naval.html.

General Register Office for Scotland. *ScotlandsPeople.* http://www.scotlands people.gov.uk/.

Inveresk (Midlothian): Records, Sources, and Information about the Parish of Inveresk and the Burgh of Musselburgh. http://www.ancestor.abel.co.uk/Inveresk.html.

Lindsay, Maurice. "James Mylne" *The Burns Encyclopedia.* [Edinburgh]: Burns Country, 1990s. http://www.robertburns.org/encyclopedia/MylneJamesd1788.672.shtml.

McNeill, Peter. *Prestonpans and Vicinity: Historical, Ecclesiastical and Traditional.* (1902; Prestonpans Historical Society, 2004). http://www.prestoungrange.org/prestonpans/html/press/vicinity/252.htm.

"Minstead Parish Council: History." *New Forest District Council.* http://www.nfdc.gov.uk/index.cfm?articleid=2364.

Moss, Michael. "Learning and Beliefs: Episcopalians." *The Glasgow Story.* http://www.theglasgowstory.com/story.php?id=TGSCC04.

"Musselburgh: East Lothian." *The Gazetteer for Scotland.* http://www.geo.ed.ac.uk/scotgaz/towns/townfirst280.html.

National Maritime Museum. "Memorial M3071." *Maritime Memorials: Commemorating Seafarers and Victims of Maritime Disasters.* http://www.nmm.ac.uk/memorials/Memorial.cfm?Search=aitchison&MemorialID=M3071.

_____. "Memorial M3072." *Maritime Memorials: Commemorating Seafarers and Victims of Maritime Disasters.* http://www.nmm.ac.uk/memorials/Memorial.cfm?Search=aitchison&MemorialID=M3072.

"Person Page 1807." *ThePeerage.com: A Genealogical Survey of the Peerage of Britain as Well as the Royal Families of Europe.* http://www.thepeerage.com/p1807.htm.

Phillips, Michael. *Ships of the Old Navy: A History of the Sailing Ships of the Royal Navy.* http://www.cronab.demon.co.uk/INTRO.HTM.

Royal Navy. *Royal Navy and Royal Marines Reference Site.* http://www.rnreference.mod.uk/.

"St Michael and All Angels: Lyndhurst." *Southern Life (UK).* http://freepages.genealogy.rootsweb.com/~villages/lyndchur.htm.

"Statistical Account of Scotland 1845: Parish of Prestonpans." *Prestonpans Historical Society.* http://www.prestoungrange.org/prestonpans/html/accounts_1845/1.html.

United Kingdom. Hampshire Record Office. Hampshire Quarter Sessions, c. 1350-1970. http://www.a2a.org.uk/.

United Kingdom. Public Record Office. Chancery: Petty Bag Office: Writ Files. http://www.combs-families.org/combs/records/england/pro/c.htm.

White, Gavin. "Glasgow." *The Scottish Episcopal Church: A New History.* http://www.episcopalhistory.org.uk/07glasgow.html.

"William Aitchison (1784-1837)." *The Usher Family of Scotland.* http://freepages.genealogy.rootsweb.com/~usher/ushersct/4009.htm.

INDEX

Italicized page numbers refer to photographs, illustrations, and caption information.

$\mathcal{G}$ENE A. SMITH, professor of history at Texas Christian University, received his Ph.D. in history from Auburn University, specializing in Jeffersonian politics and military policy. He serves as director of the Center for Texas Studies and has authored or edited numerous publications including *Thomas ap Catesby Jones: Commodore of Manifest Destiny* (Naval Institute Press, 2000); a revised and updated edition of Arsène Lacarrière Latour's *Historical Memoir of the War in West Florida and Louisiana, 1814-15, with an Atlas* (University Press of Florida in association with The Historic New Orleans Collection, 1999); and *Filibusters and Expansionists: Jeffersonian Manifest Destiny, 1800-1821*, with Frank L. Owsley, Jr. (University of Alabama Press, 1997).